Egyptian Women Workers and Entrepreneurs

Egyptian Women Workers and Entrepreneurs

Maximizing Opportunities in the Economic Sphere

Sahar Nasr, Editor

THE WORLD BANK
Washington, D.C.

1818 H Street, NW
Washington, DC 20433
Telephone: 202-473-1000
Internet: www.worldbank.org
E-mail: feedback@worldbank.org

ISBN: 978-0-8213-8190-8
eISBN: 978-0-8213-8191-5
DOI: 10.1596/978-0-8213-8190-8

Library of Congress Cataloging-in-Publication Data has been applied for.

Cover photo: Safaa Habib, the National Council for Women, Egypt
Cover design: Naylor Design, Inc.

Contents

Boxes

Figures

Tables

Foreword

Egyptian Women Workers and Entrepreneurs is a joint product of the government of the Arab Republic of Egypt and the World Bank. The report was initiated by a request from Dr. Mahmoud Mohieldin, Minister of Investment; Mrs. Aisha Abdel-Hadi, Minister of Manpower and Immigration; and Dr. Farkhonda Hassan, Secretary General of the National Council for Women.

Their request came at an opportune time. Egypt has made laudable progress in empowering women in society and in the economic sphere, but challenges remain. The World Bank Country Strategy praised Egypt's progress in reducing gender disparities and closing gaps in education, health, and economic participation, but it also noted the need for continued work and committed to assisting the government through both analytical and project support. This book forms part of that commitment.

Supporting programs that contribute to women's economic empowerment is important, as a growing body of research demonstrates the benefits to society of empowering women. Recognizing this need, the World Bank Group launched the Gender Action Plan in 2007 to promote "gender equality as smart economics." Since its inception, the plan has catalyzed activities such as this publication, both in client countries and across the World Bank Group.

The World Bank Group has been pleased to support the government of Egypt in identifying the obstacles facing women in the economic sphere. The main findings of this publication have already been integrated into the National Gender Strategy launched jointly by the World Bank, and the government of Egypt. We look forward to helping to implement this study's recommendations and hope this publication will increase attention to the role of women in the economy, ultimately contributing to leveling the playing field for women in Egypt, and maximizing their opportunities in the economic sphere.

Mayra Buvinic
Sector Director
Gender and Development
World Bank

Emmanuel Mbi
Director
Middle East and North Africa
World Bank

Zoubida Allaoua
Director
Finance, Economic, and Urban Development
World Bank

Preface

The Arab Republic of Egypt is undergoing significant demographic, social, and economic changes, including the roles of women and men. Opportunities and obstacles exist for women in the pursuit of education, livelihood, entrepreneurship, and old-age security. There is also wide scope for creative policy approaches to increase gender equity. Stemming from its belief that gender mainstreaming plays a vital role in development, the government has consistently expressed its commitment to integrating women fully into the development process.

The government's commitment to women's empowerment is strong at the highest political levels. Such commitment has been evident in identifying the empowerment of women in the Egyptian National Strategy; in mainstreaming gender in the Five-Year National Development Plan; and in establishing, by presidential decree, the National Council for Women (NCW), an official government body responsible for empowering women economically, socially, and politically and addressing their strategic needs by safeguarding their human rights. In his pledges during the 2005 presidential elections, President Hosni Mubarak highlighted the instrumental role of women in the development process.

Over the past decade, Egyptian women have witnessed significant progress in improving their status. New laws enable women to initiate divorce (*khula*) and to give Egyptian nationality to their children by non-Egyptian fathers. Specialized courts now hear all family-related issues, including custody and divorce. The first Egyptian woman judge was appointed by presidential decree—a sign of women's increased clout in decision-making circles. And the Constitution was amended to allow for a quota of female parliamentarians.

A key priority area for the government is to empower women economically by enhancing their access to markets and finance and encouraging female entrepreneurship. Equally important are the provision of support social services and the establishment of healthy working conditions, so that women employees can participate effectively in the economic sphere.

Much remains to be done to translate economic reforms into real positive changes. Promoting an enabling institutional, legal, and regulatory environment for women's equal ownership and access to economic resources and assets such as land, finance, and property is essential for economic empowerment. Freeing women and their families from poverty requires strengthening their economic capacity as entrepreneurs, producers, and informal workers so that they can access and shape markets.

The progress and pace of these gender efforts have been commended at home and abroad. But challenges and impediments remain. The government will continue to foster efforts to mainstream gender in its national social and economic plan, as well as in the budget. We hope that the findings and recommendations of this report will assist in the ongoing endeavors to meet this challenge.

Mahmoud Mohieldin
Minister of Investment
Egypt

Aisha Abdel-Hadi
Minister of Manpower and Immigration
Egypt

Farkhonda Hassan
Secretary-General
National Council for Women
Egypt

Acknowledgments

Egyptian Women Workers and Entrepreneurs is a joint product of the government of the Arab Republic of Egypt and the World Bank. The study was initiated by the Ministry of Investment, the Ministry of Manpower and Immigration, and the National Council for Women to assist in analyzing the factors influencing the low participation of women in economic activities, including the labor market and entrepreneurship.

This study was carried out under the joint leadership of Emmanuel Mbi, Country Director of Egypt, Yemen, and Djibouti Country Department; Zoubida Allaoua, Director of Finance, Economic, and Urban Development; and Mayra Buvinic, Sector Director, Gender and Development, all of the World Bank Group. It was prepared by a team led by Sahar Nasr, Lead Financial Economist, World Bank, and was based on input from Hoda Rashad, Research Professor and Director at the American University in Cairo (AUC); Heba Nassar, Vice President at Cairo University and Professor of economics at the AUC; Hania El Sholkamy, Research Associate Professor at the AUC; Naglaa El Ahwany, Professor of economics at Cairo University and Deputy Director and Lead Economist at the Egyptian Center for Economic Studies (ECES); Ramadan Hamed, Research Professor at AUC; Somaya El Saadany, Research Associate Professor at the AUC; Andrew Morrison,

Lead Economist at the World Bank; Elena Bardasi, Senior Economist at the World Bank, Carmen Niethammer, Program Officer; and Jozefina Cutura, Laila Abdel Kader, Lina Badawy, Yasmine Wissa and Mohamed El Sherif, consultants at the World Bank.

The authors are grateful to the feedback and guidance provided by the peer reviewers, Heba Handoussa, Lead Author of the Egypt Human Development report; Amanda Ellis, Lead Gender Specialist; and Andrew Stone, Lead Private Sector Development Specialist. For validation of the findings of the three surveys, the Investment Climate Surveys, the recall questionnaire, and the worker modules on which this study is based, consultative meetings, field assessments, workshops, and round-table discussions were held; a high-level policy meeting was organized, chaired by the Minister of Investment, the Minister of Manpower and Migration, and the NCW Secretary General; and a series of policy workshops were convened. Consultations were organized with various stakeholders, including businesswomen, civil society, trade unions, and donors active in the gender field. The study also draws on existing research and interviews with public and private sector stakeholders.

The Central Agency for Public Mobilization and Statistics (CAPMAS) of the Ministry of Planning provided crucial primary data on the labor market and employment. The authors thank them, as well as the many experts who provided their time and thoughts to the team conducting this study.

Abbreviations

AUC	American University in Cairo
AWTAD	Association for Women's Total Advancement and Development
CAPMAS	Central Agency for Public Mobilization and Statistics
CEDAW	Convention on the Elimination of All Forms of Discrimination
CIB	Commercial International Bank
ICA	Investment Climate Assessment
ICS	Investment Climate Survey
LFSS	Labor Force Sample Surveys
MENA	Middle East and North Africa
NCW	National Council for Women
NGO	nongovernmental organization
NILEX	Nile Stock Exchange
OECD	Organisation for Economic Co-operation and Development
R&D	research and development
SFD	Social Fund for Development
TFP	total factor productivity

All dollar figures are U.S. dollars.

Overview

Women are a powerful force for sustainable economic growth. A growing body of microeconomic empirical evidence and emerging macroeconomic analysis shows that gender inequality limits economic growth in developing economies (Ellis, Manuel, and Blackden 2006). Research also shows that considerable potential for economic growth could be realized if countries support women's full economic participation. Increases in women's income tend to correlate with greater expenditure on family welfare and children, because women often spend a greater share of their income on their children's nutrition, health care, and education. From an economic perspective, removing gender biases and maintaining a level playing field reduces possible market distortions or malfunctioning. Moreover, promoting women's participation in business may bolster women's overall participation in the labor market, because women-owned businesses are more likely to employ other women.

The potential of women-owned enterprises to employ other women is crucial for countries in the Middle East and North Africa (MENA) region, where women's labor force participation rates lag those of men. Empirical evidence shows that per capita income in MENA could have grown substantially more rapidly if women had had greater access to economic opportunities (World Bank 2004). Research suggests that 0.9 percentage points of the 1.8 percentage point annual per capita growth difference between the countries in MENA and those in East Asia and the Pacific—half the difference—can be attributed to higher initial gender inequality in education and slower progress toward closing that gap (Klasen 2002). More recent research incorporates the effect of gender inequalities in employment on economic growth. This work finds that the combined costs of the education and employment gaps have amounted to a 0.9–1.7 percentage point difference in growth between MENA and East Asia (Klasen and Lamanna 2008).

These potential benefits of gender equality are not lost on governments in the region, which have invested heavily over the past decades in social sectors, such as health, education, and training. These investments have produced generations of young, well-educated women with great potential to participate in the economic sphere. As a result, the region is closing the gap on some gender disparities, and women outnumber men at universities in 11 out of 18 countries in the Middle East (World Bank 2007d). Labor force participation, although still low compared with that in other regions, is growing rapidly.

But the surge in participation rates of workers ages 25–30 this decade, especially among educated women, has left women's unemployment two to four times higher than men's (World Bank 2007d). Moreover, women's social advancements have not always translated into their higher economic participation.

Study Methodology

This report analyzes the main reasons for this disparity in the Arab Republic of Egypt and proposes solutions to level the playing field and enable women's full economic contributions. It draws on data from the World Bank Investment Climate Survey (ICS), the ICS recall questionnaire, and a Gender Workers Module. The ICS of 1,156 enterprises from the manufacturing sector was carried out in October 2008, using the World Bank standard methodology. The recall questionnaire of 566 enterprises was conducted in October 2008. The Gender Workers Module was conducted in August 2005. It sampled about 15 full-time workers from each firm covered by the ICS recall survey. About 70 percent of the ICS sample is made up of small and medium firms, about 85 percent of which are owned by individuals or families. Large firms—firms employing more than 150 workers—account for about 30 percent of the sample. In about 35 percent of the sample, a woman is a main shareholder; in 15 percent of these firms, women own the majority of the firm.

The limitation of the ICS is that it reflects only the perspective of entrepreneurs who established firms; it does not reflect the views of those who were unable to do so because of barriers in the business environment. The main data limitation of the workers module is that it does not identify the reasons why some individuals are not able to participate in the labor force.

Progress toward Ensuring Equal Legal and Economic Status for Women

Egypt has made progress in improving women's legal and economic status, and there is a strong political commitment to women's economic empowerment. Cognizant of continued gender disparities, the government has taken steps to redress them. Commitment to women's economic empowerment is strong at the highest political level, as is evident in the president's policy statement at the Annual Conference of National Council for Women (NCW) in March 2005. In his pledges during the presidential campaign in 2005, President Hosni Mubarak highlighted the instrumental role of Egyptian women in the development process. Ms. Suzanne Mubarak, the First Lady and NCW president, has exerted immense efforts to empower Egyptian women economically, socially, culturally, and politically, as well as to promote gender equity in the workplace. Ms. Mubarak plays a leading role in empowering Arab women and influencing their status and well-being.

The prime minister reiterated this message in July 2005 at the High Level Policy Forum on the Economic Empowerment of Egyptian Women, where he announced that the new government and the NCW were developing a national gender strategy to ensure that the gender dimension would be taken into account in the comprehensive reform program. Strengthening the participation of women in economic activities has been put up front in the NCW's mandate, as executed by its Secretary General. The Egyptian authorities are keen on enhancing women's participation in the labor market as both employees and employers. Reinforcing this commitment, the government has announced the empowerment of women as one of its top priorities.

These efforts are paying off. The World Bank's Country Assistance Strategy notes improvements in women's economic empowerment in recent years.

Some of the improvements have been in the legislative arena. The constitution already guarantees equality of opportunity to all citizens in Article 8. Moreover, Article 11 notes, "the State shall guarantee the proper coordination between the duties of woman towards the family and her work in the society, considering her equal with man in the fields of political, social, cultural, and economic life without violation of the rules of Islamic jurisprudence." In recent years, Egypt has introduced new legislation to protect women's rights. Positive legislative efforts include the family tribunal law, the nationality law, the family court law, the raising of the minimum age at which a girl may marry to 18, and the measures strengthening a woman's right to divorce. These changes have helped build stronger legal rights and privileges for women and children (World Bank 2005).

In 2009, President Mubarak announced a constitutional amendment granting women a quota of 64 seats in the parliament. This initiative aims to increase the opportunities for Egyptian women to take part in political life and to ensure their representation in Egypt's highest legislative institutions.

Barriers to Women's Full Economic Participation Remain

A number of factors prevent women in Egypt from fully participating in the nation's economic sphere. They include the overall macroeconomic environment and various legal, regulatory, institutional, and cultural constraints. Egypt ratified the Convention on the Elimination of All Forms of Discrimination against Women (CEDAW) in 1981, but it included a number of reservations. Although the surge in the number of women entering the labor market over the past two decades provides some evidence of gender empowerment and positive social change, it has also been associated with rising rates of unemployment, poverty, and the economic slowdown.

Women in Egypt have entered work in higher numbers, but gender inequality in the labor market persists. Egypt has the highest difference between male and female employment in the region (UNDP 2008). Women's labor force participation rates rose from 15.4 percent in 2001 to 23.0 percent in 2006. But their unemployment rates also rose, from 19.8 percent in 2001 to 25.1 percent in 2006 (UNDP 2008). The gender wage gap is smaller in the public than in the private sector, possibly helping explain women's preference for public sector work.

Many women who do work are in the informal sector. Of the 7 million informal workers, nearly 1.1 million are female. Most female informal workers are in agriculture, which accounts for a third of all female employment (World Bank 2003). The share of women in nonagricultural employment remains very low, at about 18 percent, and it has been growing only slowly (UNDP 2008).

When women do work, they earn less than men. The disparity is especially pronounced in the private sector. As the analysis of the ICS data reveals, these differences are not related to differences in education, absenteeism, or other job performance measures, although some of the gender disparities in pay may be related to differences in the number of hours worked. Working women are also faced with a persistent perception that their marriage and family will negatively affect their work, that they are less committed to the job, that they are unable to carry out certain difficult tasks, and that they are absent from work more often than men (table 0.1).

Large firms are much more likely than small or medium firms to employ women. The probability of finding a woman in a small firm is 36 percent lower and 29 percent lower in a medium firm than in a large firm. If one controls for other factors, there is little evidence that firms that employ women or employ more women are any more or less productive than other firms. It is, therefore, difficult to justify on productivity grounds why so many firms choose not to employ a single woman or employ such a small percentage of women.

Table 0.1   Managers' Opinions on Reasons for Not Hiring Women
(percent)

Less commitment than men	18.1
Quit job more than men	11.0
Less productive than men	3.3
Less trustworthy than men	1.3
Absence higher among women than men	14.0
Same qualification as men but lower level of training	1.8
Can't work overtime or extra hours	6.8
Marriage and maternity affect her work	20.5
Work is not accurate enough	1.0
Unable to carry out hard work	14.2
Nature of work is not suitable for women	6.4
Other	1.5

Source: World Bank 2008c.

Size and Nature of Women-Owned Firms

About 20 percent of all firms in Egypt are owned by women. Women-owned firms are as well established as those owned by men (figure 0.1). They are more technologically sophisticated and more likely to export, and they employ more women than firms owned by men (World Bank 2007d). In addition, 19 percent of workers in women-owned firms have professional competencies, compared with just 16 percent in firms owned by men.

Limited Training Opportunities for Women Workers

Access to training is very limited for both men and women in Egypt, but women have fewer training opportunities than men. Almost half of firms that employ women and offer training for their employees do not train a single woman. Special incentives could help encourage firms to strengthen training for workers and ensure that women have equitable access to training opportunities.

Lack of Access to Finance

Access to finance is limited for all firms in Egypt, and very few men or women report access to any saving scheme, such as a bank account. Only 3.4 percent of the total ICS sample have checking accounts, and 6.5 percent have savings accounts. Although access to finance is a business constraint for both women and men, evidence suggests that women face higher hurdles. Twenty percent of women, compared with

Figure 0.1   Firm Size by Gender

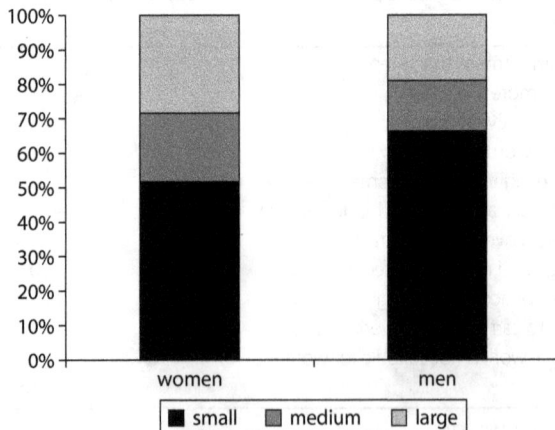

Source: World Bank 2008c.

10 percent of men, in the ICS sample consider collateral requirements a major constraint in their investment plans. The problem is even greater in the informal sector, where 33 percent of females (compared with 28 percent of males) consider collateral requirements a very severe constraint. Nineteen percent of women (compared with 9 percent of males) find loan application procedures very cumbersome.

Microcredit, which in many other countries has successfully provided finance to poor women, is not widespread in Egypt. The microenterprise sector is fragmented, with 1.3 million active borrowers. Estimates indicate that only about 5 percent of the potential microfinance market is being reached. The World Bank is designing a new project on enhancing access to finance for small and micro-enterprises in Egypt. This project offers a significant opportunity to address the gap in the provision of finance for women.

Weak Social Safety Nets for Women

Female workers in the private sector are less likely than male workers to have a work contract or social or health insurance. The gender gap is larger for contracts and health insurance (about a 10 percentage point difference) than for social insurance (about a 3.5 percentage point difference). In the public sector, the gender gap in work contracts is only about 3 percentage points, and women are more likely than men to have social and health insurance.

Lack of Physical Accommodations for Women

Workplaces often fail to accommodate the needs of women. Only about 36 percent of production lines are segregated by gender, an issue that can be crucial in a society like Egypt. Only a very small percentage of firms provide child care centers to enable women to balance their participation in economic life with their family responsibilities. These gender differences may help explain women's low participation in the labor force. They require addressing to ensure women's full economic contribution as workers.

The Need for Additional Research

Analysis of the determinants of productivity in firms finds that firms that employ more women are generally no more or less productive than other firms. Given that firms have no motivation to exclude women to increase productivity, why certain firms and sectors exclude women from employment remains unclear. Two potential explanations are (a) employing women may be more costly, because of maternity benefits or more frequent exits from the workforce to engage in child rearing, and (b) custom, prejudice, and discrimination account for the gender gap in employment. Research on the costs of employing women relative to men would help shed light on this issue and provide guidance on how best to address the disparity.

The Need for Action

The chapters that follow examine in detail issues facing women employees and entrepreneurs. They propose specific measures to redress continued disparities. The research shows that women are making significant contributions as workers and entrepreneurs in Egypt. But they have yet to reach their full economic potential and remain disadvantaged in the labor market in important ways. Whereas both male and female enterprises face high hurdles to doing business, women-owned firms perceive some constraints as more binding to their business success. In addition, hurdles outside the business environment, such as cultural constraints and norms, sometimes hinder women's economic participation. Chapter 6 proposes steps on how Egypt could tackle continued gender disparities in its labor market as well as encourage women's entrepreneurship. Implementing these recommendations to eliminate gender barriers is essential to enabling women's full contribution to Egypt's economy.

CHAPTER 1

Female Employment and the Working Environment

The government is committed to implementing all measures likely to achieve equal pay for men and women with the same job and to assist women [to] reconcile their family obligations [with] their work commitments. The government also seeks to achieve equality between men and women in all fields.

– President Hosni Mubarak,
Speech at the 35th Arab Labor Conference, February 24, 2008

Despite impressive advances in women's education, women's labor force participation rates in Egypt have been relatively stagnant and remain very low, with less than a third of women of working age in the labor force. Female labor force participation rates in the Middle East and North Africa region are among the lowest in the world; the rates in Egypt place it in the bottom third of the region. Women's participation in the labor force is associated not only with their economic empowerment, but also greater voice both within and outside the home.

Using data from the most recent labor force surveys as well as data from a 2008 survey of 1,156 workers in the manufacturing sector, this chapter provides an overview of women's participation in Egypt's labor market. The chapter analyzes the main reasons for their continued low employment levels, including salary differences between male and female workers, attitudes toward women's work, and the likelihood of receiving training and other job-related benefits.

Female Participation in the Labor Market

Egypt has a large, young, skilled labor force, in which women's share has increased over the past 30 years. Since the mid-1970s, the refined participation rate of females—defined as the share of the population age 15–64 that belongs to the labor force—has increased while the male participation rate has declined.[1] The share of women in the total labor force doubled in just two decades, rising from 7.3 percent in the mid-1970s to 15.3 percent in the mid-1990s. In 2008, the total labor force stood at 24.7 million, up from 18.7 million in 2000 and 17.0 million in 1995. The share of women increased from 22.5 percent in 1995 to 23.8 percent in 2007, with a higher percentage in rural areas than in urban areas (CAPMAS 2008). The gender gap in the labor force shrank between 1995 and 2007 in both urban and rural areas.

The labor supply is growing more rapidly among women than among men in Egypt. Female employment is growing more slowly than male employment, however, because unemployment, which reached 9 percent in 2007, continues to affect mainly the young, the educated, the rural population, and the women. Many observers believe that the real unemployment rate is higher than the official figures in 2008, given the slowdown in economic growth associated with the global economic crisis that began in 2008. Whatever the real rate of unemployment, the feminization of the phenomenon is alarming. Total female unemployment rates are nearly four times those of males (CAPMAS 2008). More than half of unemployed women in Egypt are concentrated in lower Egypt governorates, especially in rural areas, mainly because female education attainment in that region has improved, and educated rural women prefer to abandon agricultural employment and instead queue for government employment.

Women are concentrated in specific sectors, branches of economic activity, and occupations in Egypt, with the majority working as "wage earners" or "unpaid workers" (table 1.1). Most Egyptian women work in agriculture, as professionals in education and public administration, and as technicians in health and social work. In contrast, male employment is characterized by a more even distribution across sectors, activities, and occupations.

In urban Egypt, the government plays a key role in providing jobs for women. It has been the largest contributor to employment growth for

Table 1.1   Working Status of Male and Female Workers in Urban and Rural Areas, 1995 and 2007

(percent)

	1995				2007			
	Urban		Rural		Urban		Rural	
Type of worker	*Male*	*Female*	*Male*	*Female*	*Male*	*Female*	*Male*	*Female*
Wage workers	69.0	91.1	49.3	26.5	69.1	86.2	55.9	26.1
Employers using workers	12.2	1.7	25.7	8.3	11.8	1.9	20.8	4.3
Self-employed	14.7	3.5	11.6	17.3	16.0	5.8	10.7	19.9
Nonwage family workers	4.2	3.6	13.4	47.9	3.1	3.1	12.7	49.7

Source: Authors, based on data from CAPMAS 1995, 2007.

both men and (particularly) women in recent years. Its share in total female employment was 36.2 percent in 2007 (table 1.2).

Over the same period, the share of state-owned enterprises in total employment fell considerably, from 9 percent in 1995 to less than 4 percent in 2007. Private sector employment of women grew at a slower rate than government employment or employment of men in the private sector. The majority of both men and women work in the private sector (74 percent of men and 62 percent of women in 2007).

More than two-thirds of women employed in the private sector work outside establishments, most of them in agriculture and the informal sector. Agriculture is a major source of employment for women, especially in rural areas. Although the importance of agriculture declined between 1995 and 2003, this trend has started to reverse for females. Agricultural female employment increased to 43.2 percent in 2006 (CAPMAS 2008).

Informal employment doubled in a decade to reach 4.8 million in 1996, representing a third of total employment and 86 percent of nonagricultural private sector employment. Males accounted for the overwhelming majority of informal employment in trade, construction, manufacturing and transport; females in the informal sector worked mainly in education, health, social work, and household services.

Of the 8.3 million people working informally in Egypt in 2008, 1.8 million were females, representing almost half of total female employment in Egypt. Nearly 94 percent of informal female employment in the private sector is found in rural areas, with 63.9 percent concentrated in the governorates of Menia, Sharkieh, Beheira, Menofia, and Gharbieh (CAPMAS data 2008). Among female workers, 63 percent are nonwage

Table 1.2   Employment of Male and Female Workers in Public and Private Sectors, 1995, 2006, and 2007
(percent)

Sector	1995			2006			2007		
	Male	Female	Total	Male	Female	Total	Male	Female	Total
Public sector	33.5	42.5	35.3	26.5	42.1	29.5	26.1	37.8	28.6
Government	23.4	38.1	26.3	22.0	40.3	25.5	21.9	36.2	24.9
State-owned									
enterprises	10.1	4.4	9.0	4.5	1.8	4.0	4.2	1.6	3.7
Private sector	66.4	57.5	64.7	73.5	57.9	70.6	73.9	62.1	71.3
Private	65.2	56.5	63.5	72.3	57.1	69.4	72.0	61.2	69.7
Investment	0.7	0.5	0.7	0.8	0.5	0.8	1.5	0.7	1.3
Other	0.5	0.5	0.5	0.4	0.3	0.4	0.4	0.2	0.3

Source: Authors, based on data from CAPMAS 1995, 2006, 2007.

earners working for families, and a fourth are self-employed. The shares of the self-employed and wage workers are higher in rural areas, because of the dominance of agriculture (CAPMAS data 2008).

The Working Environment for Men and Women in the Manufacturing Sector

This section describes the working environment the surveyed workers face and examines whether differences between men and women are based only on gender or are explained by other differences. The focus on the working environment and gender-related differences is prompted by a number of policy concerns. One is the growing fear that in a context of high unemployment, Egypt's move toward an open market and private sector–led growth carries with it the risk of infringing on basic rights to decent and fair work conditions. Another concern is the realization that gender gaps in women's participation in public life reflect discriminatory practices not consistent with equal opportunity principles.

Egypt's Labor Law and its constitution provide for equality between men and women. Article 88 of the Labor Law states, "All employment policies and regulations should apply to female employees, equalizing their status to that of their male counterparts without discrimination as long as their work conditions are analogous." But there are certain exceptions. Article 90 states, "The concerned minister shall issue a decree determining the works that are unwholesome and morally harmful to women, as well as the works in which women may not be employed."

Both policy concerns speak to the protective role of the state and its efforts to ensure the well-being of its citizens and to combat discriminatory practices. Such concerns are not driven solely by individual-level considerations. They also find support in an economic paradigm that stipulates that a healthy work environment and increased participation of women in the market economy are engines for productivity, profitability, and economic growth (Anker, Melkas, and Korten 2003; Pérotin, Robinson, and Loundes 2003).

Characteristics of Female Workers

In the private sector, females are much younger than males (51 percent of females and 17 of males are under the age of 25), and they tend to have less work experience. About three-quarters (73 percent) of females are single, about three times the percentage (26 percent) of males. Both men and women in the private sector work mainly in small firms, as production workers.

The situation is more equal in the public sector, but there are still clear gender differences. Public sector workers are much older than those working in the private sector: 93 percent of males and 94 percent of females are at least 30 years old, compared with 65 percent of males and 27 percent of females in the private sector. Less than 9 percent of both males and females are single (table 1.3). Female workers in the public sector tend to be more educated than males: about 22 percent of females have a university degree compared with less than 16 percent of males. Women are, nevertheless, more likely to be in administrative jobs (56 percent of females and 25 percent of males hold such positions).

About 8 percent of workers in the private sector and 2 percent of workers in the public sector earn less than LE150 a month, a level of

Table 1.3   Percentage of Single Workers in Private and Public Sector Enterprises, by Age and Gender
(percent)

Age	Private sector			Public sector		
	Female	*Male*	*Total*	*Female*	*Male*	*Total*
<20	100.0	98.1	98.9	n.a.	n.a.	n.a.
20–24	97.4	84.1	89.5	66.7	85.7	80.0
25–29	79.8	46.1	53.6	66.7	78.6	76.5
30–39	30.9	8.2	10.3	8.7	11.3	10.6
40+	13.6	1.9	2.9	3.9	0.5	1.4

Source: Authors, based on the Gender Workers Module (2005).
Note: n.a. = not applicable.

compensation about equal to the upper poverty line estimated in a national study by the United Nations Development Programme (UNDP) in 2003. Low salaries are much more prevalent in private firms than in the public sector. Females are more than twice as likely as males to be poorly paid, in both the private and public sectors, with more than 16 percent of females in the private sector earning less than LE150 a month.[2]

In the private sector, men are five times as likely as women to earn at least LE400 a month. The gender differential is much smaller in public enterprises.

In both the private and public sectors, about 20 percent of employees are not compensated for overtime, with females about six percentage points more likely than males not to be compensated. Females are somewhat more likely to work more days a week than males, but daily working hours tend to be slightly longer for males (El-Kogali 2000).

Women's Contributions to Family Expenses and Responsibility for Household Spending

About half of respondents live in households in which both partners are responsible for daily spending. Female respondents claim to be responsible for daily spending more often than male respondents. Divergence in their perceptions may reflect imperfect correspondence between groups (female respondents are not necessarily the wives of male respondents).

Eighteen percent of married women in the Investment Climate Survey report that relatives or other people rely on them to satisfy their needs, including their living expenses. The load is lighter for unmarried women, 3.6 percent of whom report that others rely on them to satisfy their needs. Among male respondents, 13.3 percent report contributing to satisfying the needs of others who do not live with them, mainly by contributing to dependents' expenses.

Single women make significant contributions to family expenditures. Almost 70 percent report making contributions, of which 17.8 turn over their entire income to their family and another 29.7 percent give at least half their earnings.

The majority of married women are parallel rather than secondary family breadwinners. Among married women, 3.4 percent are the sole breadwinner in the family and 61.8 percent provide half or more of their families' total income. Among women who were never married, 6.9 percent are the sole breadwinners in their families, and 26.8 percent provide at least half their family's income.

Attitudes of Men and Women toward Women Working

Women do not appear to work primarily out of necessity: 54 percent of women report that they would still work even if there were no need for them to do so (table 1.4). Most of those who would stop working would do so because "work is hard." Religious reasons were not cited as an important factor for not working.

The most important factor motivating women to work is a high salary. Gender-specific factors, such as the presence of a daycare facility, are not among the most important motivators (table 1.5).

Men's attitudes toward women's work are not very positive, with only 13 percent of men affirming that women should work. The main reason

Table 1.4   Primary Reasons Women Work
(percent)

Reason for working	Percentage of female respondents citing factor as most important
To contribute to family's expenses	34.8
For myself	21.9
For protection and security	19.5
To contribute to marriage expenses	14.5
To contribute to children's expenses	9.3
Would continue to work if didn't need the money	53.8

Source: Authors, based on data from the Gender Workers Module (2005).

Table 1.5   Primary Factors Affecting Women's Decision to Accept a Job
(percent)

Factor	Percentage of female respondents citing factor as most important
High salary	18.7
Respected job	17.5
Well treated at work	15.9
Proximity to home	9.4
Fixed salary	8.9
Good transportation	7.3
Working hours	7.3
Insurance in public sector	2.9
High position	2.4
Support husband/family	2.2
Existence of daycare	2.2
Little work	1.4
Child was grown	1.1
Only female workers	0.1
Other	2.7

Source: Authors, based on data from the Gender Workers Module (2005).

men want women to work is so that they can contribute to household expenses (table 1.6); the main reason men do not want women to work is their belief that women need to take care of their children (table 1.7).

Resistance to Employing Women

More than half of managers in the sample indicated that there was no advantage to employing women workers. About 18 percent said that women have

Table 1.6   Primary Factors Affecting Husband's Decision to Accept Wife Working
(percent)

Factor	Percentage of married male respondents citing factor as most important
Nature of wife's position	
Wife earns high salary	10.7
Wife earns high salary and does not have young children	4.3
Wife has respected job and earns fixed salary	4.2
Wife has respected job and earns high salary	3.4
Wife earns fixed and high salary	3.1
Wife does not have young children	2.8
Wife has respected job and earns fixed and high salary	1.9
Wife earns fixed and high salary and has good hours	1.9
Wife earns fixed salary	1.8
Wife earns high salary and has good working hours	1.7
Wife earns fixed salary and does not have young children	1.6
Use of income	
Contributes to family's expenses	26.5
Contributes to family's and children's expenses	17.4
For herself	14.6
For herself and family expenses	7.1
Other	9.1

Source: Authors, based on data from the Gender Workers Module (2005).

Table 1.7   Main Reasons Husband Does Not Want Wife to Work
(percent)

Reason	Percentage of married male respondents citing factor as most important
Needs to take care of children	26.8
Needs to take care of children and "I don't like her working"	21.4
"I don't like her working"	18.9
"Didn't find opportunity"	7.1
Children and "didn't find opportunity"	5.7

Source: Authors, based on data from the Gender Workers Module (2005).

high productivity and are committed to work. In the Middle East and North Africa region, there is evidence that women entrepreneurs hire more women workers (box 1.1). When asked to list the disadvantages of hiring women, respondents cited domestic duties and marriage (49 percent), family responsibilities (43 percent), and absenteeism (33 percent). As for potential solutions to enable women to overcome these obstacles, 40 percent of respondents said there was no solution, 23 percent mentioned flexible working hours, and 13 percent mentioned nurseries.

Box 1.1

Women in the Middle East and North Africa Region Employ More Women

Workers in female-owned firms are as educated and as skilled as those in male-owned firms. Except in Lebanon and Saudi Arabia, female-owned firms employ more women than do male-owned firms. This is true not only in Morocco and Syria, where female-owned enterprises are most prevalent in the traditionally female textile sector, but also in Egypt and the Republic of Yemen, where male- and

Female Workers Hired in Male- and Female-Owned Firms

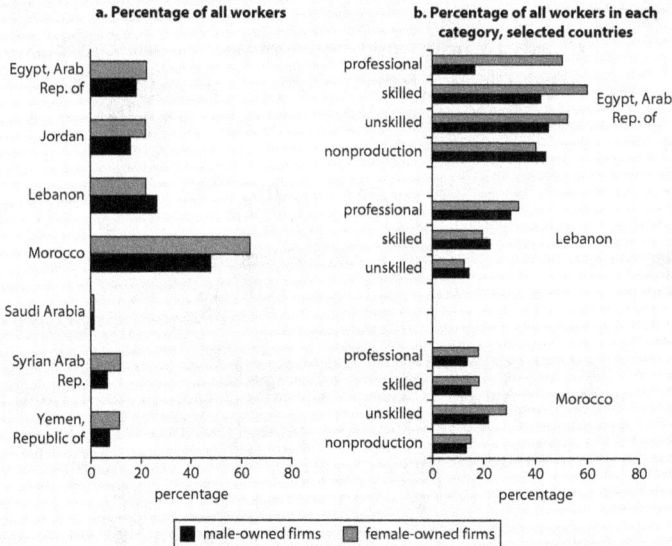

Source: World Bank Enterprise Survey data 2003–06.

(continued)

Box 1.1 *(continued)*

female-owned firms are distributed similarly across sectors. Female-owned firms in Egypt and Morocco not only hire a higher proportion of female workers than do male-owned firms, but they also employ a higher share of female workers at professional and managerial levels. This finding is particularly relevant given the high unemployment of highly educated women in the region. Promoting female entrepreneurship can thus be a tool for fostering women's participation in the labor market and for reducing the unemployment of highly educated women.

Finally, female-owned firms are hiring more workers in general. Except in the Republic of Yemen, the direction and the extent of workforce changes in female-owned firms is as good as or better than that in male-owned firms. In Egypt, Jordan, Saudi Arabia, and the West Bank and Gaza, the share of female-owned firms that have increased their workforce recently exceeds the share of male-owned firms that did so, and fewer female-owned firms than male-owned firms have decreased their workforce.

Source: Chamlou, Klapper, and Muzi 2008.

Job Benefits

Roughly two-thirds of both men and women report working for firms that provide annual leave (table 1.8). The use of job benefits (annual leave, casual leave, sick leave, and so forth) is fairly similar among women and men.

Egypt's Labor Law guarantees maternity leave and two daily break periods for all nursing mothers. If a company hires more than 100 women, it is also required to establish a daycare facility. It is unclear what share of companies comply with this provision or how well it is being enforced, but there is anecdotal evidence that the requirement is leading companies to employ fewer than 100 women (Bakir 2005). Forty percent of female workers surveyed stated that their firm does not provide maternity leave, and more than half indicated that there is no child care leave. These factors may help explain the high levels of single female workers in the private sector.

The percentage of employees receiving training in managerial and administrative skills is higher among women, and the percentage of employees receiving training in production is higher among men (table 1.9). For all employees, the probability of receiving any kind of

Table 1.8   Job Benefits Provided and Used by Women and Men at Sampled Firms
(percent)

	Women			Men		
Benefit	*Benefit exists*	*Request to use benefit made*	*Company honored request*	*Benefit exists*	*Request to use benefit made*	*Company honored request*
Annual leave	67.3	82.7	99.7	68.8	85.6	99.5
Casual leave	65.3	78.3	99.7	65.3	79.3	99.3
Sick leave	75.1	69.6	100.0	74.4	72.3	99.6
Maternity leave for women	59.8	38.6	100.0	n.a.	n.a.	n.a.
Childcare leave for women	46.8	26.5	100.0	n.a.	n.a.	n.a.
One-hour permission (for nursing mothers)	52.0	33.3	100.0	n.a.	n.a.	n.a.

		Among firms offering training		Probability of receiving training (across all firms) (percent)[a]	
	Firms offering training (percent)	*Percentage of all women employed that received training*	*Percentage of all men employed that received training*	*Women*	*Men*
All firms	20.4	5.6	14.7	1.1	3.0
Firms employing no women	5.6	n.a.	26.7	n.a.	1.5
Firms employing both men and women	14.7	14.7	14.8	2.2	2.2

Source: Authors, based on data from CAPMAS 2008.
Note: Within the sample, 412 firms had no female employees, and 741 firms employed both men and women in 2006; 236 firms in the sample offered training; of these, 65 had no female employees, and 171 employed both men and women. n.a. = not applicable.
a. Defined as the percentage of firms offering training times the percentage of workers receiving training in firms that offer training.

training is higher among professionals and administrative staff than among other workers. The majority of sampled employees reported benefiting from training and wanting to receive more of it.

Gender-Related Differences in Job Types, Salaries, Promotions, Appointments, and Travel

Between one-quarter and one-third of employees perceive gender differences on a range of career issues, including appointments, travel,

Table 1.9   Types of Training Offered
(percentage of employees receiving training, except where otherwise indicated)

Type of training	Received training (percentage of all employees of same gender)	Last time training offered	Certificate received	Improved job skills (scale 1–4)	Improved position	Wants more training
Female respondents						
Training on new machines/ production	3.3	2002	36.8	2.9	47.4	36.8
Training in management or administrative skills	3.9	2001	80.0	3.2	76.0	76.0
Education opportunities	4.0	2000	84.6	2.8	61.5	84.6
Male respondents						
Training on new machines/ production	3.9	1999	47.3	3.2	61.3	52.7
Training in management or administrative skills	2.3	2000	78.7	3.1	60.7	75.4
Education opportunities	1.6	1997	86.0	2.9	62.8	74.4

Source: Authors, based on data from CAPMAS 2008.

promotion, and salaries (the figure is higher among women than among men) (figure 1.1). About two-thirds of all workers perceive a gender distinction regarding the type of jobs women and men perform. These clear gender differences in the perceived treatment of male and female workers warrant addressing. Chapter 6 provides suggestions on doing so.

Male workers earn more than female workers, especially in the private sector (table 1.10). As analysis of the Investment Climate Survey data reveals, these differences are not related to differences in education, absenteeism, or other job performance measures. Some of the gender disparities in pay may be related to differences in the average number of hours worked per week and skill levels; however, both of which are higher among men.

Figure 1.1   Male and Female Employees' Perceptions of Gender Differences in Salaries and Work Benefits
(percentage of employees perceiving differences)

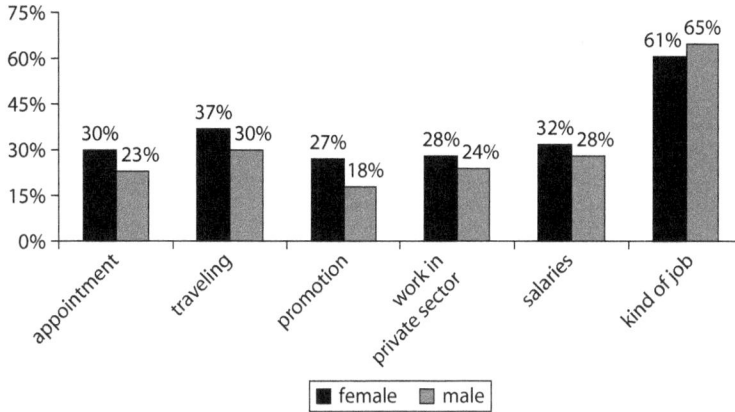

Source: World Bank 2008c.

Table 1.10   Monthly Salaries of Workers at Private and Public Sector Enterprises, by Gender
(percent)

Monthly salary (LE)	Private			Public			Total
	Female	Male	Total	Female	Male	Total	
<100	2.6	0.8	1.1	0	0	1.1	0.9
100–150	13.8	5.2	6.8	4.8	1.3	6.8	5.9
151–200	22.2	7.5	10.2	10.5	11.0	10.2	10.2
201–300	36.6	24.1	26.4	25.7	25.0	26.4	25.7
301–400	16.4	22.1	21.0	21.0	24.0	21.0	20.9
400+	8.4	40.4	34.4	38.1	38.7	34.4	36.4

Source: Authors, based on data from CAPMAS 2008.

There are fewer gender differences in pay increases, promotions, or other related benefits. Male employees are slightly more likely than female employees to enjoy pay increases and other benefits, but the difference is small (an exception is pay cuts, which are more likely to affect women but which are infrequent overall). Among women in the sample, 74 percent had had a pay increase over the year preceding data collection and 37 percent had received a bonus. However, more than 95 percent had not received a promotion or learned any new production skills, and just 9 percent had received any work-related training or education. The rates were similar for male workers.

Notes

1. The crude participation rate of women increased between 1995 and 2007.
2. A 2005 study estimates that women earn 78 percent as much as men (JICA 2005). This figure may not represent discrimination, however, because, on average, women have less experience and fewer skills than men and spend less time working.

CHAPTER 2

Women's Entrepreneurship

The empowerment of women and their acquisition of professional skills have also enabled them to pierce through the job market acceding to managerial positions. Today, women's identity and their potential are being valued by society as well as internationally.

– H.E. Mrs. Suzanne Mubarak, First Lady of Egypt, President of the National Council for Women, and President of the Suzanne Mubarak Women's International Peace Movement, April 2007

The role of the private sector in development has increased significantly over the past decade, and so has the participation of women in private sector activities, as both employees and employers. Worldwide, registered women-owned enterprises account for one-quarter to one-third of all businesses in the formal economy, and the figure is often higher in the informal sector (World Bank Enterprise Surveys database).

Enhancing women's participation in entrepreneurship is essential for improving national welfare, because establishment of businesses not only generates income for women's families, but also creates jobs for men and women alike. It helps reduce unemployment, a key challenge in the Middle East and North Africa. Reducing unemployment is crucial for Egypt, where economic reforms and privatization have led to the shrinking of the public sector, which has traditionally employed a larger share of women than men. Because the private sector has not been able to absorb the women's growing labor force, encouraging women to start their businesses and become employers rather than job seekers is a crucial strategy for job growth in Egypt.

Women's Ownership of Firms

About 20 percent of companies in Egypt are owned by women (World Bank 2007d). Women-owned firms are as well established as those owned by men (figure 2.1) and are more likely to be in the nondurable manufacturing sector. Women-owned companies account for 45 percent of all textiles and garment firms, 20 percent of chemical and pharmaceutical industry firms, and 15 percent of firms in the food industry (World Bank 2008c). Businesses in the durable sectors, such as furniture and metallurgic industry firms, are more likely to be owned by men.

Women-owned firms also tend to be more technologically savvy than firms owned by men, more likely to be located in the capital, and more likely to use the Internet, as well as more likely to be exporters than

Figure 2.1   Size Distribution of Firms Owned by Men and Women in Egypt

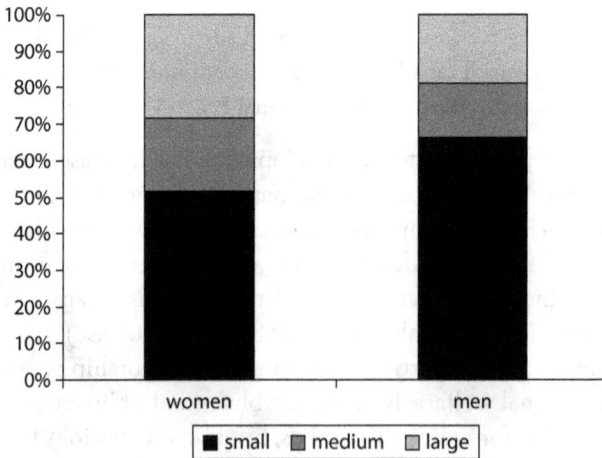

Source: World Bank 2008c.
Note: Large firms are defined as those employing more than 100 workers, medium firms as those employing 50–100 workers, and small firms as those employing 10–49 workers.

male-owned firms (World Bank 2007d). Small firms owned by women are more likely to employ other women.

Improvements in the Business Environment

Egypt recognizes the key role the state plays in providing the enabling environment that facilitates private sector development. It has made great strides in improving its business environment, as evidenced by its outstanding performance in the World Bank's annual *Doing Business* survey. Egypt implemented 22 reforms to its business environment between 2003 and 2008 alone. In 2007/08, it further reduced business registration costs and its minimum paid-in capital requirement. Reforms have also been carried out to facilitate business start-up and credit provision. In addition, Egypt has implemented one-stop shops for import and export and business start-up. It has introduced tax reforms, improved its credit information systems, and modified the listing rules of the Cairo Stock Exchange (World Bank 2008b). Despite these improvements, the country lags behind several others in the region. It ranked 106th among 183 economies in the *Doing Business 2010* report (table 2.1). Its worst-performing areas were dealing with construction permits (156th), enforcing contracts (148th), and paying taxes (140th).

Table 2.1   Egypt's Rankings in *Doing Business 2010*

Doing business area	Rank
Having ease of doing business	106
Starting a business	24
Dealing with construction permits	156
Employing workers	120
Registering property	87
Getting credit	71
Protecting investors	73
Paying taxes	140
Trading across borders	29
Enforcing contracts	148
Closing a business	132

Source: World Bank 2009a.

Different Constraints Facing Male and Female Entrepreneurs

Although male and female entrepreneurs operate in the same environment and deal with the same institutions, the challenges they face sometimes differ (figure 2.2). Some impediments in the business environment—corruption, transportation, licenses, and permits—affect men and women entrepreneurs equally.

Others seem to affect women more than men. Both women and men rate macroeconomic uncertainty as their greatest constraint (the figure is somewhat higher for women). Female-owned firms are more likely to perceive access to land and electricity as constraints. They report a yearly average of 40 percent more power interruptions and losses of sales caused by power outages or surges from the public grid. They also report greater legal constraints than do male-owned firms—an average of eight months longer to resolve disputes over overdue payments (World Bank 2007d).

At the same time, women-owned firms rate labor regulations as a less severe constraint, possibly because they are more likely to comply with them. Women-owned firms report higher losses as a result of these problems (7 percent of total sales compared with 5 percent for male-owned firms) (World Bank 2007d).

Figure 2.2   Percentage of Firms Rating Constraint as Major or Severe

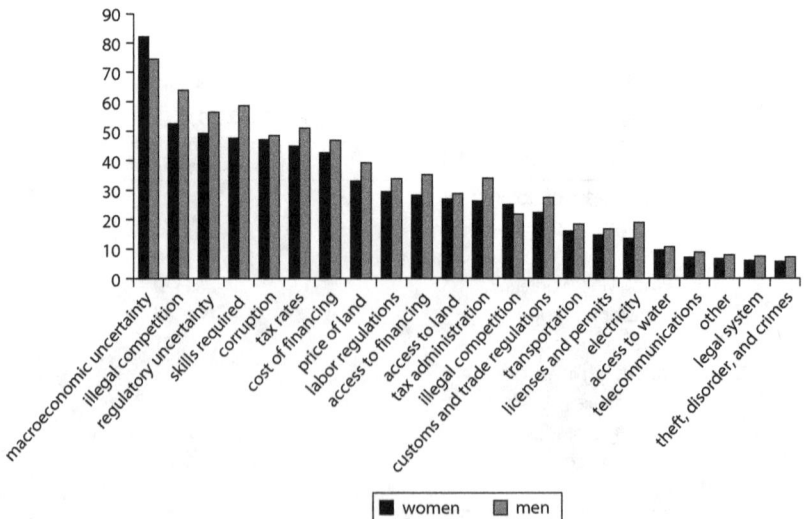

Source: World Bank 2008c.

Box 2.1

Women's Time Use in Africa

Women in many countries work longer than men. In Ghana, for example, women's time burden is 20–25 percent higher than men's (Awumbila and Monsen 1995). In Kenya, women work 12.9 hours per day, compared with 8.2 hours for men. Despite their longer hours, they earn less than men, because more of their hours are unpaid (Saito, Mekonnen, and Spurling 1994). In Tanzania, time spent on household chores such as fetching water and collecting firewood represents a significant constraint on women's ability to run off-farm businesses. Women in the Kagera district spend 10 hours a week collecting firewood and water. Reducing that time by one hour increases the probability of women engaging in off-farm business by 7 percent (Mduma 2005).

Women's participation in business is often hampered by family responsibilities. Women are the main caregivers in Egypt, and they spend more time on household activities, reducing the number of hours they can allocate to productive and income-generating activities. This situation is especially pronounced in parts of Egypt where there is a lack of good-quality social services, such as childcare centers. In this respect, Egyptian women's time constraints are similar to those of women elsewhere in the world (box 2.1).

In addition to having less time for economic pursuits, women in Egypt often perceive their earnings as a means to complement family income. Most of those surveyed do not have plans for important changes or strategies for expanding their businesses (World Bank 2008c).

Women entrepreneurs in Egypt are constrained by mobility issues. As a result of cultural norms and traditions, some women are prevented from traveling alone, which limits their effectiveness as entrepreneurs. Women workers in the Investment Climate Survey sample highlight the difficulties of getting to work. Almost 40 percent of those whose firms do not provide transport reported facing difficulties getting to work. (Improving transportation is one of the major recommendations of surveyed workers discussed in chapter 6).

Organizations Fostering Women in Business

There has been an increase in organizations catering to the interests of women in business According to the *Egypt Human Development Report,*

Box 2.2

Nurturing Women's Businesses: The Example of AWTAD

Set up in 2007, the Association for Women's Total Advancement and Development (AWTAD) has been part of the growing wave of associations targeting the needs of women in business in Egypt. According to its Web site (http://www.awtadegypt.org/), the association aims to "empower and engage the community, to mobilize the role of women as nucleolus development agents, through effectively leveraging Egypt's social and human capital." Its activities are tied to the perceived needs of Egyptian women. They include a Steps into the Future Mentoring Program, a breast cancer awareness program, a corporate ambassadors program, and business education e-learning.

The association has been well received by men. According to Shereen Allam, one of AWTAD's cofounders and a successful business owner, "A lot of men want to be members. Men have applied because they say they believe in the cause. They say, 'We will give our time and efforts for free to promote the association.' One great man said, 'I owe everything I have to my mom. I want to contribute to the cause.'"

The association is part of a regional network sponsored by Vital Voices (a U.S.–based nongovernmental organization [NGO]) and the U.S. Department of State. Members of the network exchange information and advice and provide ideas on appropriate activities for women in their region.

about $42.2 million in international aid was directed toward programs to promote gender equality and empower women in 2004, representing 5.7 percent of total foreign assistance in Egypt. Educational programs received 47 percent of this aid; the health sector received 7 percent.

Several dozen women's business associations operate in Egypt. They include the Association for Women's Total Advancement and Development (box 2.2), the Egyptian Business Women Association, the Alexandria Business Women Association, Business Women 21, the Businesswomen Association for Development, the Development of Businesswomen Export Ability Association, the Egypt-based Arab Women Investors Union, and the Women in Business Committee of the American Chamber of Commerce (Al-Ayram Weekly 2007). These groups can play a critical role in helping grow women's businesses. They can also raise awareness of the broader issues facing women in business, such as legislative obstacles or potential barriers to women's participation in the labor force.

CHAPTER 3

Labor Markets, Firm Productivity, and Gender

Although Egyptian women's economic participation has been growing in recent years, they still have limited access to the labor market . . . The privatization and free market policies led to the shrinking of the public sector—the main employer of women; and at the same time, the private sector did not step in to employ women.

– National Council for Women,
Beijing +10. National Council for Women, Cairo

This chapter examines the position of women in Egyptian manufacturing firms, using data from the World Bank's Investment Climate Survey (ICS). It documents the degree of labor market segregation by gender in Egypt, presents regression results on the factors affecting women's employment, and analyzes the effect of gender segregation on productivity in manufacturing.

Occupational and sectoral segregation refers to the concentration of men and women in different occupations and productive sectors. If workers are distributed across sectors and occupations as a result of custom, prejudice, and discrimination rather than because of productive characteristics that influence labor demand or voluntary choice on the part of workers, allocative inefficiency may result.

Many authors have suggested that women are willing to accept lower wages in exchange for job characteristics such as flexible work schedules or the ability to combine work with childcare (Fain 1998; see also Polachek 1981; Filer 1985). If this tendency is the case, much of what is labeled as occupational segregation is, in fact, women's voluntary choice. The debate between voluntary and nonvoluntary explanations for segregation has not been fully resolved. Occupational segregation is associated with less job security, fewer prospects for advancement, and lower wages for all workers (Anker and Hein 1986). Allowing women access to nontraditional sectors and occupations may raise both productivity and incomes.[1]

Sex Segregation in Egypt

Analysis of the ICS reveals a pattern of sex segregation in Egypt's manufacturing firms, where women are underrepresented as both workers and managers. Female workers represent about 21 percent of all workers in the economy. In no occupational group do women represent less than 19 percent (professionals and managers) or more than 22 percent (skilled workers) of all workers. Given this lack of variation in the presence of women in different occupations, there seems to be very little occupational segregation. Female workers are overrepresented in textile industries and underrepresented in the engineering, metal, and building industries (table 3.1).

Table 3.1   Composition of the Investment Climate Survey Sample
(percent)

Firm characteristic	Firms	Workers	Female workers
Sector			
Agroindustries	1.3	—	—
Chemicals	7.5	1.9	0.5
Electronics	0.6	51.5	62.9
Garments	11.2	15.8	13.9
Machinery and equipment	3.3	5.4	1.4
Metal industries	16.3	2.5	0.4
Nonmetal industries	11.5	4.2	1.6
Textiles	16.7	18.7	19.3
Other	31.5	—	—
Size			
Small (10–49 employees)	53.5	6.1	5.7
Medium (50–99)	17.0	8.4	7.2
Large (100+)	29.6	85.4	87.1

Source: World Bank 2008c.
Note: — = not available.

Forty-one percent of the firms in the sample (403 of 988 firms) employ only men (figure 3.1). Two-thirds of the firms in the sample (665 of 988) have no female managers or professionals. About the same proportion (675 of 988) have no women in skilled positions.[2]

The median firm's labor force is 8.7 percent female; only the top 10 percent of firms (ranked by percentage of women employed) have equal numbers of women and men (table 3.2). The median firm employs no female managers or professionals; at the top 10 percent of firms, at

Figure 3.1   Composition of Firms' Labor Force by Gender and Occupation

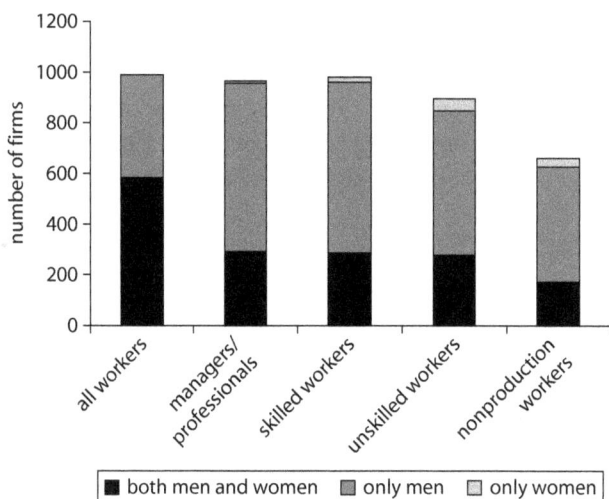

Source: Authors, based on World Bank 2008c.

Table 3.2   Sex Segregation by Firm Percentile

Indicator	Percentile of firms				
	10th	*25th*	*50th*	*75th*	*90th*
Percent women	0	0	3	20	100
Percent female professionals	0	0	0	4	20
Percent skilled workers	0	0	0	5	40
Percent female unskilled workers	0	0	0	3	22
Percent female nonproduction workers	0	0	0	0	6

Source: World Bank 2008c.
Note: These percentiles were applied on the number of female workers. The data indicate that the first 25 percent of firms do not employ women (0 for 10th and 25th percentiles). Up to the 90th percentile, firms employ women (100 percent in the 90th percentile means that at the 90th percentile, all firms employ women). For those exceeding the 90th percentile, all firms would definitely be employing women (since it is already 100 percent on the 90th percentile). If we assume that the number of female workers indicates the size of the firm (which is a valid assumption), then the largest firms (which are the remaining 10 percent) will all be employing women.

least 40 percent of all managers are women. Skilled workers are even more unequally distributed, with no woman in this category in more than half of all firms. Women represent more than three-quarters of skilled workers at the 10 percent of firms, however, and at least 40 percent in the top 20 percent of firms.

Despite this heterogeneity among firms, at the economywide level the representation of women across occupations is on average remarkably equal (table 3.3) (see box 3.1 for information on how women's share by occupation was computed).

The role of women in firms varies across sectors. The share of women among managers/professionals in the textile (about 15 percent) and food (8 percent) sectors is smaller than the overall share of female workers in these two sectors; in other sectors, the reverse is true. In the textile industry, which absorbs the largest number of female workers of any sector, the percentage of women among unskilled workers is higher than in other sectors. In all firms there is an overrepresentation of unskilled women.

Certain sectors are more likely to employ women than others. About 52 percent of machinery and equipment enterprises and 39 percent of garment enterprises employ women. By contrast, only 15 percent of

Table 3.3   Percentage of Female Workers, by Occupation and Sector

Firm characteristic	All workers	Managers/ Professionals	Skilled workers	Unskilled workers	Nonproduction workers
Sector					
Agroindustries	13.26	7.95	11.89	18.72	8.66
Chemicals	20.46	25.10	21.35	26.78	15.29
Electronics	19.78	28.05	6.93	19.17	45.42
Garments	44.91	28.36	50.75	42.44	26.18
Machinery and equipment	10.59	20.01	5.89	12.37	24.34
Metal industries	5.56	9.39	3.85	6.51	7.97
Nonmetal industries	6.22	10.95	6.26	4.92	13.94
Textiles	21.88	14.68	24.33	26.60	11.85
Other	14.85	14.48	13.18	20.49	17.85
Size					
Small (10–49 employees)	15.36	10.97	16.16	16.46	12.18
Medium (50–99)	19.25	18.47	17.95	25.37	20.51
Large (100+)	19.36	22.56	19.18	23.78	18.04
All	17.21	15.85	17.36	20.34	15.85

Source: World Bank 2008c.

Box 3.1

Computing the Share of Women by Occupation

The percentage of women in each occupation j is computed as

$$Pw_j = \frac{\sum\limits_{i=1}^{N} w_{ij} \cdot h_i}{\sum\limits_{i=1}^{N} n_{ij} \cdot h_i},$$

where w_{ij} is the number of women in firm i ($i = 1 \ldots N$) and occupation j ($j = 1-4$); n_{ij} is the total number of workers (male and female) in firm i; and occupation j and h_i are firm weights (based on number of employees and other factors).

agroindustry businesses and 32 percent of enterprises in the metal and wood sectors employ women.

The presence of women is also related to firm size. Almost 45 percent of large firms but only 29.5 percent of small firms and 42.2 percent of medium-size firms hire women (table 3.4). This result is not surprising, because even if the probability of hiring a woman were constant across firms of different sizes, the probability that a large firm hired a woman would be higher because of the larger number of employees.

Factors Affecting the Probability of Employing Women

Several models of the probability of employing women were estimated. Columns (1)–(5) in table 3.5 show the marginal effects of various firm characteristics on the probability of employing at least one woman (column 1), at least 20 percent women (column 2), at least 33 percent women (column 3), at least 40 percent women (column 4), and at least 50 percent women (column 5). For columns (1)–(5), a probit model was estimated with a zero-one dependent variable (either the firm employs a woman or it does not, either it employs at least 20 percent women or it does not, and so forth).[3] For column (6), a fractional logit regression model was estimated (Wooldridge 2002) to explain the proportion of women employed by firms. The fractional logit model is appropriate when the dependent variable is a proportion that is defined only in the interval $[0,1]$ and can take the extreme value of 0. The results are reported

Table 3.4   Presence of Women in Enterprises, by Sector

Indicator	Percentage of firms employing women
Sector	
Agroindustries	15.4
Chemicals	28.8
Electronics	42.9
Garments	39.3
Machinery and equipment	51.7
Metal industries	31.7
Nonmetal industries	30.5
Textiles	37.4
Other	35.6
Firm size	
Small (10–49 workers)	29.5
Medium (50–99 workers)	42.2
Large (100+ workers)	44.5
All	34.9

Source: World Bank 2008c.

in column (6) in the form of odds-ratios.[4] The probability that a firm employs women in a professional or managerial occupation was estimated using a probit regression model (see column (7)).

In addition to firm size and sector, the regressions include firm characteristics, such as the degree of competition; the age of the firm; the ownership structure; whether the firm exports its product or service; and innovation/technology variables, such as the presence of a research and development department, the use of foreign technology, the adoption of technology since 2003 that substantially changed the production process or introduced new products, whether the firm obtained an internationally recognized quality certification, and whether the firm offers internal or external training.

The multivariate analysis indicates that sector and firm size are the most consistently significant variables related to the presence of women in the firm. They also have some of the largest marginal effects of all explanatory variables.

Large firms are much more likely than medium and small firms to employ women. The probability of finding a woman in a small firm is 36 percent lower than in a large firm; in a medium-size firm, the probability of finding a woman is 29 percent lower than in a large firm. Small firms are significantly less likely than large firms to have a workforce that has more than 20 percent but less than 40 percent women; there is no

Table 3.5 Probability of Employing Women and Female Professionals

Variable	Employs women (1)	Employs >20 percent women (2)	Employs >33 percent women (3)	Employs >40 percent women (4)	Employs >50 percent women (5)	Percent women employed (6)	Employs women as professionals/managers (7)
Size (base = firms with 100+ employees)							
Small (<50 employees)	-0.465	0.129	-0.298	-0.491	-0.374	0.628	-1.633***
Medium (50–100 employees)	0.006	0.196	-0.984	-1.193*	-0.470	1.006	-0.165***
Sector (base = textiles)							
Chemicals	-0.017	-0.498	-0.485	-0.432	-0.408	0.983***	1.153*
Electronics	-0.918	-21.248	-20.595	-20.188	-20.817	0.399	1.359
Food	-2.436**	-21.513	-20.154	-19.860	-20.428	0.088***	-0.606
Garments	0.778	0.882	1.156**	0.766	0.518	2.178	1.258**
Machinery	-2.489***	-1.668**	-20.792	-20.448	-20.083	0.083***	-0.020
Metal industries	-1.609***	-2.542***	-2.407***	-2.374***	-2.358***	0.200	0.178
Nonmetal industries	-2.108***	-2.280***	-2.495***	-2.185**	-2.957**	0.121***	-0.152
Other	-1.235***	-1.242***	-1.478***	-1.594***	-3.037***	0.291**	0.204
Number of competitors (base = more than 20)							
No competitors	-2.183***	0.548	-0.015	1.120	1.725	0.113	-0.953
1–5 competitors	-1.202*	0.700	0.789	1.459	0.822	0.301**	-0.316
5–20 competitors	-0.270	1.029	1.316	1.737	1.342	0.763	-0.037
Competitor is import	-0.347	0.990	0.097	1.182	0.539	0.707	0.431
Do not know	-0.646	1.193	0.952	1.544	0.961	0.524	0.055

(continued)

Table 3.5 Probability of Employing Women and Female Professionals (Continued)

Variable	Employs women	Employs >20 percent women	Employs >33 percent women	Employs >40 percent women	Employs >50 percent women	Percent women employed	Employs women as professionals/ managers
	(1)	(2)	(3)	(4)	(5)	(6)	(7)
Age of firm (base = before 1990)							
Recent (1990–99)	-0.349	-0.380	-0.333	0.010	-0.200	0.706**	-0.052
New (2000 and after)	-1.310***	-1.152**	-1.473	-1.352**	-1.069	0.270	-0.786*
Ownership structure (base = individual)							
Family	0.290	0.153	-0.082	-0.415	-0.316	1.336	0.280
Dummies							
Has owner who is female	0.557*	0.656**	0.400	0.345	0.765	1.745	0.233
Exports part of product	0.592	0.572	-0.608	0.467	-0.760	1.807***	0.597
Received quality certification	0.411	0.269	-1.154*	-1.486**	-0.756	1.509	0.649
Has research and development department	1.097**	0.135	-0.534	-0.055	-0.301	2.994*	0.465
Uses foreign technology	0.505	0.203	1.157*	1.006	0.125	1.656	0.437
Has a generator	-0.092	-0.671	-0.256	-0.316	-0.658	0.912	-0.265
Offers training	0.553	1.047***	1.444***	1.158**	1.902***	1.738**	0.037
Cox and Snell R^2	0.287	0.257	0.182	0.181	0.182		0.276
-2 log-likelihood	351.936	311.209	139.069	205.756	139.069		356.205
Correct percentage predicted	0.749	0.786	0.919	0.881	0.919		0.769

Source: Authors, based on data from World Bank 2008c.

Note: Sample size is 346. Marginal effects are reported in columns (1)–(5) and (7). For dummy variables, the marginal effect is the change in the predicted probability when the dummy changes from 0 to 1. Odds ratios are reported in column (6).

***Significant at the 1% level; **significant at the 5% level; *significant at the 10% level.

difference among firms of different sizes in the probability of employing more than 40 percent women.

Large firms are more likely to employ women in managerial and professional roles. This probability is 30 percent higher than in small firms and 11 percent higher than in medium-sized firms.

As in many other countries in Africa and Asia, the textile sector is the most likely sector to employ women. All sectors are significantly less likely to employ women than men: 21–23 percent less in the food and chemical sectors, 42–45 percent less in the wood and engineering sectors, 52 percent less in the metal sector, and 61 percent less in the building and construction sector. Firms in the textile sector are also much more likely than other firms to employ a large proportion of women. They are 6–11 percent more likely than firms in the food, chemical, metal, and building and construction sectors to have a majority female workforce.

Foreign-owned firms are more likely than their domestic counterparts to employ women, including as professionals. Foreign firms are about 30 percent more likely to employ women. Family-owned firms are slightly more likely to have a high percentage (40–50 percent) of female employees. Women-owned firms are significantly more likely (16 percent more likely) than other firms to employ women in professional and managerial roles.

A range of technology variables (quality certification, research and development [R&D] department, adoption of new technology) do not seem to matter in terms of employing women. New firms (defined as firms created after 1999) are 10–12 percent more likely to employ a substantial portion of women than older firms.

Gender Composition and Productivity

As the analysis above shows, a high percentage of firms employ only men; many other firms employ only a small percentage of women. Is this rational behavior on the part of firms? Are they employing few women because women are less productive than men? Or are they not hiring equally productive women in order to satisfy what economists call a "taste for discrimination"?[5]

To investigate this question, we estimated a Cobb-Douglas production function:

$$\ln V_i = \beta_0 + \sum_{j=1}^{7} D_{ij}(\alpha_{jL} \ln L_i + \alpha_{jK} \ln K_i) + \varepsilon_i, \tag{3.1}$$

where V_i is the value added for firm i (defined as the value of the total output, measured by total sales minus the value of intermediate materials); L_i is the number of employees; K_i is the capital stock, proxied by the replacement value of land, buildings, and production equipment; and D_i are sector-specific dummies that allow the coefficients of labor and capital to be sector specific. Total factor productivity (TFP) is then constructed as the estimate of ε_i, the part of the value added that is not explained by sector affiliation, capital, and labor.[6]

To check the robustness of the results, we also estimated a production function with total output as the dependent variable (total value of sales) and labor, capital, and intermediate materials as explanatory variables:

$$\ln Y_i = \beta_0 + \sum_{j=1}^{7} D_{ij}(\alpha_{jL} \ln L_i + \alpha_{jK} \ln K_i + \alpha_{jM} \ln M_i) + \varepsilon_i. \qquad (3.2)$$

TFP is once again calculated as the estimate of the residual. The results of the estimation of the production functions are reported in the annex.[7]

Controlling for other factors, we find little evidence that firms that employ women or employ more women are any more or less productive than other firms (figure 3.2). It is, therefore, difficult to justify on productivity grounds why so many firms choose not to employ women.

To decrease the noise caused by the small number of firms in each decile, we examined the same figures by quintiles (figure 3.3). The results are very similar: in the top quintile of TFP, there is a lower percentage of women (and in particular a lower percentage of women in skilled occupations) than in the lower quintiles. Women in professional and managerial occupations are an exception; for these women, there is no relationship with either the TFP quintile or decile.

To check whether these results are robust to the inclusion of other explanatory variables that could be related to TFP, we estimated the following regression:

$$TFP_i = \gamma_0 + \gamma_1 X_i + \gamma_2 Z_i + v_i, \qquad (3.3)$$

that is, we regressed TFP in firm i on a vector of firm-specific characteristics X_i and a vector of "segregation measures" Z_i that captures the presence or absence of women in the firm. We ran several regressions with different specifications of the segregation measures (table 3.6). The first specification (a) includes the proportion of women in the firm, as well as the proportion of professionals/managers and the proportion of skilled workers who are

Figure 3.2   Percentage of Women in Various Occupational Groups, by Decile of Total Factor Productivity

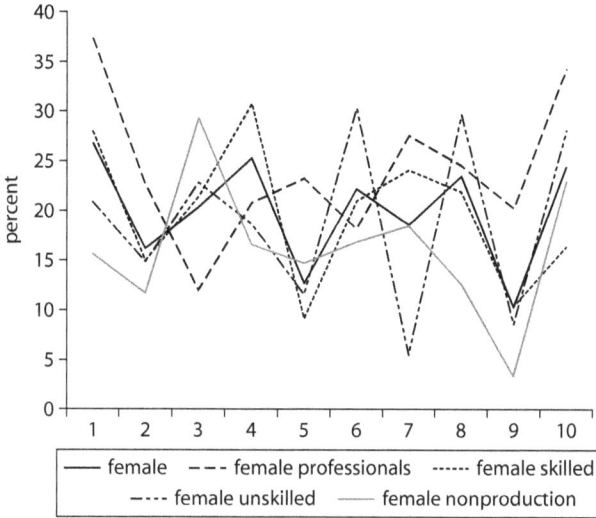

Source: Authors, based on data from World Bank 2008c.

Figure 3.3   Percentage of Women in Various Occupational Groups, by Quintile of Total Factor Productivity

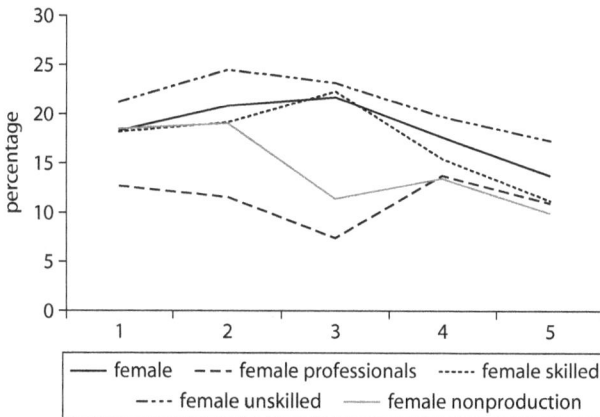

Source: Authors, based on data from World Bank 2008c.

women. Specification (b), (c), and (d) use 0/1 dummy variables for having at least a certain percentage of women, female professionals/managers, and female skilled workers in the firm. Using a value added production function (equation 3.1), we find that the estimated segregation coefficients are never statistically significant, suggesting that firms employing women

Table 3.6   Impact of Female Employees on TFP

Explanatory variable	Type of production function estimated at first step	
	Value added (equation 3.1)	Total output (equation 3.2)
(a) Percentage women	0.001	0.001
Percentage professional women	0.023***	0.022***
Percentage skilled women	−0.005	−0.005
(b) At least 50 percent women	−0.038	0.007
At least 50 percent professional women	0.360	0.481
At least 50 percent skilled women	−0.166	−0.292
(c) At least 40 percent women	0.131	0.082
At least 40 percent professional women	0.483*	0.543**
At least 40 percent skilled women	−0.108	−0.157
(d) At least 33 percent women	0.299	0.253
At least 33 percent professional women	0.494**	0.588***
At least 33 percent skilled women	−0.291	−0.365

Source: Authors.
Note: The regressions control for the degree of competition; the age of the firm; the ownership structure; the firm's export orientation; and innovation/technology variables such as the presence of an R&D department, the use of foreign technology, the adoption of technology since 2003 that substantially changed the production process or introduced new products, whether the firm obtained an internationally recognized quality certification, and whether the firm offers either internal or external training. TFP = total factor productivity.
***Significant at the 1% level; **significant at the 5% level; *significant at the 10% level.

(specification a) or a larger percentage of women (specifications b–d) are no less productive than firms employing only men.

The results are similar using the total output production function (equation 3.2). The majority of coefficients are not statistically significant. There are, however, two exceptions: firms in which women make up at least half of the labor force are 26 percent less productive than firms employing a smaller percentage of women (or no women at all), and firms in which at least a third of the workforce is female are estimated to be 16 percent less productive than other firms.

Because firms with and without women in their workforce could have very different characteristics, we also tested the robustness of our findings using a propensity score matching model to compare the TFP of firms with and without women.[8] Firms employing women are about 8 percent more productive than similar firms that do not employ women, but the difference is not statistically significant and the two groups of firms do not differ significantly in their average level of TFP.[9]

Annex

Production Function Estimates

Table 3A.1   Production Function Estimates

Item	Value added	Total output (sales)
Labor * garments	0.263	0.529
Labor * textiles	0.163	0.213
Labor * machinery	0.515	0.348
Labor * chemicals	0.464**	0.203
Labor * electronics	−0.382	0.642
Labor * metal	0.133	−0.051
Labor * nonmetal	0.384**	−0.058
Labor * food	1.197	0.773
Capital * garments	−0.091	0.120
Capital * textiles	0.061	0.051
Capital * machinery	−0.070	−0.067
Capital * chemicals	−0.127	−0.272
Capital * electronics	0.229	1.880
Capital * metal	0.101	0.046
Capital * nonmetal	−0.082	−0.120
Capital * food	−0.575	−0.082
Materials * garments	—	−0.309
Materials * textiles	—	−0.002
Materials * machinery	—	0.122
Materials * chemicals	—	0.248
Materials * electronics	—	−1.292
Materials * metal	—	0.154
Materials * nonmetal	—	0.285 *
Materials * food	—	−0.069
Constant	7.096***	7.899***
Number of observations	627	671
R-squared	0.099	0.120

Source: Authors, based on data from World Bank 2008c.
Note: — = not available.
***Significant at the 1% level; **significant at the 5% level; *significant at the 10% level.

Notes

1. This is a testable hypothesis: with good wage data, one can analyze whether women in traditionally "female" occupations earn less than women with similar sociodemographic characteristics in nontraditional occupations. This analysis can be done using econometric techniques that model the decision to participate in the labor force and choose occupations (double selection models; see Pitts 2003) or statistical techniques that construct matched groups of women working in female-dominated and nonfemale-dominated

occupations (matching models; see Lamanna and Morrison 2006). If women in female-dominated occupations earn more than those in nontraditional occupations, the nonvoluntary segregation explanation can be rejected. The converse is not also true: lower earnings in nontraditional occupations are consistent with both voluntary choice and social custom, prejudice, and discrimination. Because the main ICS questionnaire did not collect wage data, this type of analysis was not undertaken in this chapter.

2. From the initial size of the sample we dropped firms with missing or implausible numbers of workers. We were left with a sample of 988 firms that spanned seven industrial sectors (food, chemicals, metals, wood, textiles, building, and engineering).

3. In a probit regression, the regression coefficients are difficult to interpret. Thus, in columns (1)–(5) and (7) of table 3.5, the marginal effects (that is, the effect of a one-unit change in independent variables on the probability that a firm employs a woman) are reported.

4. A coefficient greater than 1 should be interpreted as a positive effect (1.2 indicates that the effect is 20 percent greater); a coefficient less than 1 should be interpreted as a negative effect.

5. Most models of "discriminatory tastes" assume that firms can engage in such tastes only if market imperfections give firms some monopoly or oligopoly power in product markets. If firms have no such power, these models predict that competition will drive these firms out of business because their discriminatory practices make them less efficient than firms that do not discriminate.

6. This is the same estimation procedure used in the Egypt ICS (World Bank 2005).

7. In both estimations, we estimated the studentized residuals—a statistical term, denoting a residual divided by its own standard deviation—to reduce the effect of outliers (see Bollen and Jackman 1990) and discarded the observations with residuals with absolute values greater than 2. This method resulted in dropping 40 observations when the estimation of TFP is based on the value added production function and 49 observations when it is based on the total output production function.

8. Matching of firms with and without women in professional and managerial occupations was unsuccessful, because very few controls were available to be matched in the upper part of the propensity score distribution.

9. These results are very similar if we perform the matching on small firms only. The difference in TFP between firms with and without women is about 15 percent (lower in firms with women), but the difference is not statistically significant. Because of the small sample size, propensity score matching could not be performed for medium and large firms.

CHAPTER 4

Women's Access to Finance

Financial exclusion is likely to act as a "brake" on development as it retards economic growth and increases poverty and inequality. However, the access dimension of financial development has often been overlooked, mostly because of serious data gaps on who has access to which financial services.

> – Asli Demirguc-Kunt, Senior Research Manager, Finance and Private
> Sector Development, Development Research Group,
> World Bank, 2007

Egypt's banking sector is dominated by public sector ownership, a lack of competition, a reluctance of banks to lend, and the underdevelopment of nonbank financial institutions. Market-based financial intermediaries play a limited role. There has been a decline in the overall provision of credit in the Egyptian economy in recent years, as indicated by the sharp decline in private credit as a share of GDP, which fell from 65 percent in 2003 to 40 percent in 2008, and a decline in the loan-to-deposit ratio, which fell from 70 percent to 50 percent over the same period (World Bank 2009b). The recent financial crisis has exacerbated the problems that businesses, especially small and micro-enterprises, face in accessing finance.

Egypt's government is aware of these issues and is undertaking major reforms to improve macroeconomic fundamentals, restructure the financial sector, and increase market capitalization. Facilitating private sector development by improving financial sector competitiveness and efficiency and promoting equity are among the key strategic objectives in Egypt's Country Assistance Strategy. Efforts on this front have included implementation of the Financial Sector Reform Program, issuance of the Small Enterprise Law 141 of 2004, creation of the Small Enterprise Development Organization under the Social Fund for Development, and endorsement of the National Microfinance Strategy in 2005. In addition, in 2008, the Central Bank of Egypt issued a decree reducing reserve requirements for lending to small firms. The Central Bank of Egypt approved the establishment of a Small Enterprises Unit at the Egyptian Banking Institute in 2008 to provide capacity building to banks. The launching of the small Nile Stock Exchange (NILEX) in 2008 was meant to facilitate small firms' access to equity capital. These steps are positive, but it will take some time for them to trickle down and affect entrepreneurs.

The Limited Role of Formal Financing

Formal financing plays a limited role in financing enterprises in Egypt: only 7 percent of new investment and working capital is financed through the banking sector, compared with more than 13 percent in the region, 18 percent worldwide, and 60–70 percent in most Organisation for Economic Co-operation and Development (OECD) countries (World Bank 2009a). Despite ongoing reforms, state-owned banks continue to dominate the banking system. They lag in efficiency and are slower to adapt to change than private sector banks (World Bank 2007a). The problem is evident in the *Doing Business 2009* rankings, in which Egypt ranked 84th out of 181 economies in the getting credit category; its performance improved the following year, to 71st, following positive reforms (World Bank 2008a, 2009c).

Liquidity constraints often force entrepreneurs to rely on internal funding or retained earnings. Commercial banks are reluctant to lend to start-ups. Banks view them as risky, because it is difficult to assess their viability and credit worthiness, especially when they are small.

Although access to finance is a business constraint for both men and women, evidence suggests that women face higher hurdles. Women's access to finance, especially at the small and medium enterprise level, is a major constraint to their ability to start and expand businesses. As the analysis below demonstrates, women face tighter constraints in terms of the cost of and access to finance.

Lack of collateral is one major hurdle for women. The ICS shows that 92 percent of loan application rejections are based on the lack of acceptable collateral. Women are twice as likely to complain about collateral requirements as men (World Bank 2008c). Women perceive collateral requirements as a greater burden: 20 percent of women (and 10 percent of men) in the ICS sample consider these requirements a major constraint on their investment plans. The problem is even greater in the informal sector, where 33 percent of women (and 28 percent of men) consider collateral requirements a very severe constraint. Women are also more likely than men to find loan application procedures cumbersome: 19 percent of women (and just 9 percent of men) consider the process very cumbersome.

One obstacle that prevents women from putting up needed collateral is their lack of secure land rights. Egyptian law gives women ownership and inheritance rights: under *Sharia* law, women have the right to inherit half of what men inherit. Despite this provision, women make up only 5.7 percent of landholders in Egypt (World Bank 2003), and norms and customs often prevent them from managing the assets they own, which are often under the guardianship of a brother, husband, or son. To ensure that land stays within the family, families also often encourage daughters to marry relatives (World Bank 2003). As a result, women are often deprived of using their property as collateral for loans, limiting their ability to participate as independent agents in private sector activity. The survey shows that 92 percent of loan application rejections are based on the lack of acceptable collateral, a major constraint for women.

The Limited Role of Banking, Targeted Initiatives for Women, and Microcredit

Very few Egyptians—men or women—report access to saving schemes, such as a bank account: only 3.4 percent of the total sample surveyed in the Investment Climate Survey (ICS) reported having checking accounts; another 6.5 percent reported having savings accounts. These figures are higher among single women, almost 10 percent of whom have checking or saving accounts. Single women who work contribute substantially to their marriage trousseaus, taking on many of the financial burdens that had been shouldered by parents (Al-Bassusi and El-Kogali 2001).

Few women approach commercial banks for credit: only about 20 percent of female entrepreneurs go to commercial banks for credit, partly because they deem this activity too risky. Those that approach banks are confronted with higher rejection rates than men face (3.8 percent compared with 2.8 percent for men).[1] Women are more active in the informal credit market than men and are more likely to borrow funds from family and friends (Nasr 2008).

Commercial banks in many countries have recognized the business potential of their female clients (box 4.1). Progress has been slower in Egypt, where only a small number of banks specifically target women. One such program is run by the Commercial International Bank (CIB) Egypt. The bank's businesswomen's club sponsors information-sharing seminars on investing. CIB also launched a MasterCard for female customers, called Heya, although the program targets predominantly wealthy women and has limited regional reach.

Despite initiatives such as those by CIB, banks in Egypt do not systematically collect sex-disaggregated portfolio information. As a result, they lack a good understanding of the needs of women as potential customers.

Box 4.1

Targeting Female Customers: Standard Chartered Bank in Africa

Recognizing the business imperative of addressing gender issues, Standard Chartered—a global bank with a presence in more than 70 countries—has made women a key part of its business strategy. It is a member of the Global Banking Alliance for Women, a global consortium of banks that have successfully leveraged the women's market for profit.

Cognizant of women's high repayment rates in microfinance, the bank has committed to provide $500 million to microfinance institutions by 2011, a goal it is on track for meeting. Women make up 80 percent of clients in the bank's microfinance portfolio.

In Botswana, Ghana, Nigeria, Tanzania, Uganda, and Zambia, the bank's Diva Club offers women special lifestyle benefits, such as discounts at health clubs, restaurants, and beauty salons. Its Diva Chamma account encourages women to save together in investment clubs. The Diva Club in Nigeria facilitates networking among the bank's female customers. It also provides financial literacy training, which the bank is planning to provide to thousands of women in the coming years.

Source: Cutura 2009.

Microcredit, which has successfully provided finance to poor women in many countries, is not widespread in Egypt. The microenterprise sector in Egypt is fragmented, with 1.3 million active borrowers—a small fraction of the estimated 21 million poor and "near poor" people in Egypt of productive age. Matters are even worse in more remote areas. Governorates in Lower Egypt, for example, have a penetration rate for microfinance of only 3.5 percent (World Bank 2009b).

Of the numerous banks in the Egyptian banking sector, only four—the National Bank for Development, Banque du Caire and Banque Misr (recently merged), the Principal Bank for Development and Agricultural Credit, and CIB—serve the micro, small, and medium enterprise market, in which women's businesses predominate. Most private banks do not focus on this segment, which they perceive as too risky or better relegated to the government, NGOs, or the Social Fund for Development (SFD). SFD is the leading national program for small and micro-enterprises. As of March 2009, it provided finance to 208,220 microenterprises and 98,564 small enterprises by financing 435 NGOs that then on-lend these funds. The potential universe of borrowers—there are 2.3 million formally registered small and micro enterprises alone—is far larger.

Banks provide some financing to small firms, but the Central Bank of Egypt reports that the volumes amount to less than 1 percent of total loans (World Bank 2009b). Some small organizations have met with success in reaching borrowers (box 4.2). The unmet need for such services remains large, however.

Box 4.2

Facilitating Women's Access to Microloans: The Al Tadamun Microfinance Program in Egypt

In response to the need for credit by poor women, one of Egypt's most prominent microfinance organizations, Al Tadamun, was established in 1996, as a project of Save the Children. In 2003, Al Tadamun began operating under the legal umbrella of the Women's Health Improvement Association and became a Grameen-Jameel partner. The organization has served more than 60,000 female microentrepreneurs in the Greater Cairo area. Its loans are used mainly for income-generating activities, such as agriculture, shopkeeping, animal husbandry, and other cottage industries.

Source: Grameen Foundation (http://www.grameenfoundation.org/).

Figure 4.1   Use of Various Savings Vehicles, by Level of Educational Attainment

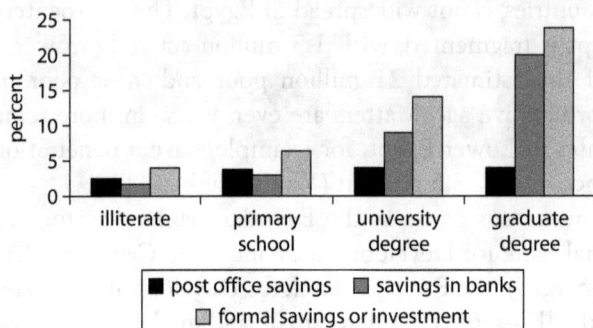

Source: World Bank 2009b.

The Need for Education and Financial and Business Management Training

There is a strong link between education and the use of savings vehicles in Egypt, with usage increasing substantially with educational level (figure 4.1). Households headed by a university degree graduate or those with a graduate degree are much more likely to have formal savings or investments and savings in banks than households headed by those who are illiterate or have only primary school education.

There remains a large need for business training among female entrepreneurs (IFC 2007). Women are often not identified as target groups for technical training, and cultural and social restrictions, as well as time constraints, often make it difficult for them to attend training courses that are offered.

Some commercial banks, such as the Bank of Alexandria and Banque Misr, are beginning to see the benefits of providing business skills training to enhance the management performance of small and medium enterprises owned and managed by women. This training, which some banks provide for their preferred women customers as part of their membership services, not only helps women acquire better financial management skills, but also enables commercial banks to interact with their female clients and reduces the credit risk for the banks.

The Need for New Reforms

Egypt's government has undertaken a number of reforms to expand access to credit information and enhance the information infrastructure. Reforms have allowed for the establishment of private credit bureaus and the sharing of credit information with nonbank financial institutions. The private credit bureau iScore is expected to improve the quality of information and reduce the cost of obtaining credit information in Egypt (World Bank 2007a). Such reforms are usually associated with improved access to finance, particularly for small and medium enterprises and women (Ellis, Manuel, and Blackden 2006).

At the request of the government, the World Bank is designing a new project. The Enhancing Access to Finance for Micro and Small Enterprises project aims to unblock the expansion of microfinance by providing additional funds through the SFD to eligible NGOs; to improve the governance of NGOs through innovative approaches to delivering and recovering loans on a commercial basis in an efficient and cost-effective manner and transforming them into profitable microfinance institutions; to help microenterprises become formal small enterprises; to engage banks in sound small enterprise lending, through both provision of support services and complementary funding to their own deposits; and to ensure gender equality in access to finance.

This project offers a significant opportunity to address the gap in the provision of finance for women. Women already make up 74 percent of active clients of SFD–supported NGOs in microfinance (World Bank 2009b). This figure is much lower in SFD's small enterprise portfolio, indicating an area in need of further attention. Integrating gender-specific concerns from the design stages through implementation by putting in place gender-specific targets and ensuring that women are designated as beneficiaries of any training and technical assistance will be crucial to enabling women to benefit from the program.

Note

1. These percentages were acquired from the question "What is the reason for not having a loan currently?" Of those responding, 2.8 percent of male principal owners and 3.8 percent of female principal owners said "Because the last application for a loan was turned down."

CHAPTER 5

Social Safety Nets, Security, and Gender

Women's empowerment is smart economics because you can show the benefits throughout the society.

> – Robert B. Zoellick, President, World Bank, March 2008

Less than a third of women in the Middle East and North Africa region are active participants in the labor force (World Bank 2007d). This rate is the lowest of any region in the world (comparable rates are 80 percent in East Asia and the Pacific, 70 percent in Europe and Central Asia, and 65 percent in Sub-Saharan Africa).

With women's labor force participation rates so low, the vast majority of women in the region either have no social security or have coverage only through their husbands. This chapter analyzes the Investment Climate Survey (ICS) firm and worker modules for gender-based patterns of provision of contracts and the availability of social safety nets in Egypt.

Work Contracts

There are three types of contracts in Egypt, with different provisions of rights:

- Regular appointments provide social insurance and strong protection against layoffs. In the public sector, they are reserved for authorized positions characterized by a permanent employment status.
- Contractual appointments (temporary or renewable) provide social insurance. They can be terminated at the end of the contract period.
- Task contracts (daily remuneration or honoraria) need not provide social insurance.

Forty-five percent of sampled workers in the manufacturing sector are not covered by a work contract. The figure is lower in the public sector (29.7 percent) than in the private sector (48.5), but even there it is significant (table 5.1).

The connection between having a contract and receiving benefits is not straightforward in Egypt, where many workers who do not have contracts report receiving social or heath insurance (table 5.2). The survey did not probe this inconsistency. Possible interpretations of these findings include

Table 5.1   Share of Workers at Private and Public Sector Enterprises without Job Benefits or Job Stability
(percent)

Item	Private	Public	Total
No work contract	48.5	29.7	43.9
No social insurance	23.1	3.4	19.5
No health insurance	27.8	3.2	23.4
No sense of job stability	25.5	16.5	25.2

Source: World Bank 2008c.

Table 5.2   Share of Workers under 30 without Work Contracts, Social Insurance, or Health Insurance, by Gender
(percent)

Item	Female	Male
No work contract	76.6	61.9
No social insurance	38.5	42.2
No health insurance	49.5	45.7

Source: World Bank 2008c.
Note: Sample includes workers under 30 who have worked at private firms with less than 100 employees for less than 10 years.

the tendency in Egypt not to provide a hard copy of the contract to employees as well as the many types of contractual arrangements.

There is a great deal of confusion surrounding the issuance of contracts in the public sector and major problems in contractual practices in the private sector. The public sector provides social and health insurance to more than 96 percent of its workers, although the recent trend toward less than full coverage of insurance is a cause for concern. In contrast, the private sector denies about a quarter of its workers such basic benefits: 23 percent of workers lack social insurance, and 28 percent lack health insurance. The situation is worse for young workers, who are even less likely to have coverage. Workers at small firms (firms employing no more than 100 workers) are less likely to have either a work contract or social insurance (tables 5.3 and 5.4).

Female workers in the private sector are less likely than male workers to have a work contract or receive social or health insurance. The gender

Table 5.3   Characteristics of Workers at Private and Public Sector Enterprises without Work Contracts

(percent)

Characteristic	Private	Public	Total
Firm size (number of employees)			
10–100	54.8	37.9	53.5
100–299	29.7	30.4	27.9
300+	28.9	28.8	28.7
Age			
Less than 20	75.3	0	74.9
20–24	64.6	20.0	60.7
25–29	48.1	29.4	46.5
30–39	40.4	30.9	37.4
More than 40	41.2	29.7	36.4
Work experience			
Less than 10 years	53.9	25.0	51.2
More than 10 years	39.6	30.2	35.4
Type of work			
Production	53.3	32.3	48.7
Nonproduction	49.8	28.2	45.5
Administration	29.7	28.0	29.0
Education			
Low (did not complete preparatory school)	55.5	29.0	50.3
Medium (did not complete university)	47.7	31.1	43.3
High (university or more)	31.9	27.1	31.2
Number of observations	1,195	1,210	1,423

Source: World Bank 2008c.

Table 5.4   Characteristics of Workers at Private and Public Sector Enterprises without Social Insurance
(percent)

Characteristic	Private	Public	Total
Firm size (number of employees)			
10–100	26.0	20.7	25.8
100–299	15.5	7.2	14.0
300+	12.4	1.0	5.9
Age			
Less than 20	57.0	n.a.	56.8
20–24	39.3	20.0	37.6
25–29	22.5	0.0	22.1
30–39	14.4	6.4	12.7
More than 40	14.7	2.1	10.5
Work experience			
More than 10 years	31.6	9.6	30.2
Less than 10 years	9.2	2.5	6.9
Type of work			
Production	22.8	5.2	19.9
Nonproduction	25.4	2.6	21.9
Administration	21.0	1.5	15.8
Education			
Low (did not complete preparatory school)	24.7	5.3	21.4
Medium (did not complete university)	21.1	2.4	17.6
High (university or more)	26.0	2.9	21.5
Number of observations	568	14	628

Source: World Bank 2008c.
Note: n.a. = not applicable.

gap is larger for contracts and health insurance (about a 10 percentage point difference) than for social insurance (where the gap is about 3.5 percentage points). In the public sector, the gender gap in work contracts is small (about 3 percentage points) and favors women for both social and health insurance. The pattern of differentials confirms the existence of slightly more favorable conditions for men in the private sector and for women in the public sector.

The relation between a contract or social insurance and an employee's sense of job stability varies by type of firm. In the public sector, the lack of a work contract is not a good indicator of employees' sense of job stability: although 29.7 percent of respondents do not have a contract, only 16.5 percent do not feel their jobs are stable. Conversely, the availability of social insurance is not enough to prevent employees from the sense that they lack job stability: about 16.5 percent of surveyed workers do not feel they have job stability, although only 3.4 percent lack social insurance. Uncertainty regarding job stability in the public sector could be linked to the nature of contracts or to the increased privatization of public firms. In the private sector, the percentage of workers who do not feel their jobs are stable is much smaller than those working without a contract but is very close to the percentage not having insurance.

Lack of Separate Physical Accommodations for Women in the Workplace

One issue that affects women's perceptions of their safety and their ability to work is the lack of separate accommodations, an important issue given cultural and social norms in Egypt. Only about 36 percent of production lines are segregated by gender. Although more than a third of enterprises have a room for male workers to use to eat and rest during their time off, only 8 percent have a rest and recreation area especially for women (5 percent have unisex spaces). Sixty percent of enterprises have no such space at all.

Although the number of working women with infants or small children in this sample was small, the firm questionnaire revealed some interesting observations on nurseries in enterprises. Firms are required by law to provide a nursery if they have more than 100 female employees. Just 16 sampled firms, all of them large firms, had nurseries (10 in the public sector, 6 in the private sector). Seven of the firms were large employers of women (more than 40 percent of their total workforce female).

None of the other firms provided a nursery or allowed flexible working hours. Ninety-two percent of women said that their place of employment does not have a nursery. With such a high share of women workers noting that they have no nurseries at work, it appears that the legislation on the matter is not being fully enforced.

Although the legislation on nurseries is meant to protect working mothers, experience from countries such as Chile suggests that it may act as a disincentive to hiring female workers. Legislation in Chile mandates that firms with 20 or more female workers must provide childcare for their working mothers or subsidize its cost. Women's labor force participation rate has remained low in Chile: at 37 percent, it is among the lowest in the region (World Bank 2007b). The law—intended to facilitate better management of women's work and family responsibilities—may have had had unintended consequences, reducing firms' incentives to hire more than 19 women.

Research indicates that one of the most serious obstacles to work-force participation cited by women is sexual harassment and discomfort at the workplace (Assad 2002; El-Mahdi 2005). Few women in the ICS sample reported that they had been harassed or molested, however. When asked how they had been harassed, they mentioned gossip and actual sexual harassment.

In contrast to these results, a survey by the Egyptian Centre for Women's Rights finds that sexual harassment is widespread in Egypt (Abdelhadi 2008). This survey finds that 62 percent of men admitted to harassing women and 82 percent of women reported having experienced sexual harassment. The center campaigned for legislation to curb the problem, which was introduced in parliament in 2009 (Abdelhadi 2008).

It is unclear why the response rate in the ICS sample is so different from the figures reported elsewhere. The discrepancy could reflect the reluctance of women surveyed to report the issue rather than the lack of the problem.

Union Membership

A relatively small percentage of employees in Egypt belong to unions (table 5.5). As a result, workers do not have access to the benefits of collective action or to credit. Only 11 percent of women workers are members of a union; among men the rate is slightly higher (16 percent). About 94 percent of all union heads are men.

Table 5.5   Union Membership among Manufacturing Workers, by Gender
(percent)

Item	Female	Male
Union membership	11.0	16.0
Firm-level representative body	17.2	14.0
Membership in body	55.9	65.8
College fund	21.2	16.6
Participation voluntary	43.8	63.8
Benefit from fund	39.4	38.8

Source: Authors, based on World Bank 2008c.

CHAPTER 6

Enhancing Women's Participation in Economic Activities: The Way Forward

Break the cycle of dependency by empowering individuals with the knowledge, skills and opportunity they need to participate in building a better life for themselves, for their families and their communities—giving them the freedom to make choices and develop their potential to the fullest.

– H.E. Mrs. Suzanne Mubark, First Lady of Egypt, President of the National Council for Women, and President of the Suzanne Mubarak Women's International Peace Movement, September 2006

As the preceding chapters demonstrate, women are making significant contributions as both workers and entrepreneurs in Egypt. But they have yet to reach their full economic potential, and they remain disadvantaged in the labor market in important ways. Although both male and female entrepreneurs face high hurdles to doing business, female entrepreneurs perceive some constraints as more binding to their business success than do male entrepreneurs. In addition, hurdles outside the business environment, such as cultural constraints and norms, sometimes hinder women's economic participation. Eliminating such barriers is essential to enabling women to fully contribute to Egypt's economy. This chapter proposes several recommendations on how Egypt could tackle continued gender disparities in its labor market and encourage women's entrepreneurship.

Continuing to Improve the Business Environment

The government has a key role in providing an enabling environment that facilitates private sector development for both women and men. Recent reforms have improved entrepreneurs' perceptions of the investment climate in Egypt and their potential for expansion, leading to greater confidence and less uncertainty. Continued reforms to reduce the costs of starting and operating businesses are likely to benefit both male and female business owners. Such reforms would help women in particular, as regions with lower start-up capital and lower exit barriers have higher shares of female entrepreneurs in the formal sector (World Bank 2007c). Although this book is a good starting point, further research is needed to gain a better understanding of the main constraints facing women and identify their priorities for reform.

Addressing Norms, Traditions, and Legal Discrimination

The degree of job segregation in Egypt remains high in some sectors. Some jobs and professions are still male dominated and viewed as inappropriate for women. The belief that men, as the traditional breadwinners, are more deserving of jobs is widespread and may be contributing to women's low labor force participation rates. Addressing social norms about working women and promoting an environment in which women can balance work and family commitments is crucial for leveling the playing field for women. Changing established norms takes time. Initial steps could include promoting nontraditional educational opportunities for girls, such as engineering or computer science.

Although progress has been made in leveling the playing field for women, some laws continue to discriminate against women. Well-intended but discriminatory provisions—such as Article 9 of the labor law, which states that women's employment may be restricted in areas considered "unwholesome and morally harmful"—should be repealed. If maternity costs are discouraging firms from employing women, the government should consider covering these costs rather than requiring individual firms to do so, thereby removing this potential disincentive to hiring women. Women's legal advocacy organizations can help provide training to judges and other judicial staff to ensure that recent legislation guaranteeing women's rights is enforced. They can also help educate women on the legal rights they have but may not be fully aware of.

Encouraging Women to Join the Labor Force

Workers perceive certain barriers to women's work as especially high. The Investment Climate Survey sample reveals that proximity to home, good transport, suitable work hours, and good pay are the top four features that would encourage women to work (table 6.1). Investing in infrastructure, such as accessible roads or an affordable urban transportation system, is therefore essential to support women's work and family responsibilities.

Improving Employment Conditions for Female Workers

Basic features of a healthy work environment include clear contractual arrangements (arrangements that specify the duration terms of employment and the rights and responsibilities of employees); fair compensation; provision of social and health insurance, fringe benefits, leave, and entitlements; and a safe and human physical environment. A work environment that is appreciative and supportive of its work force is characterized by investment in its human resources, recognition of good performance, and lack of stereotyping. Many of these features are lacking in Egypt's firms. This situation adversely affects both employees' and employers' well-being.

Despite the high unemployment rate in Egypt, there is anecdotal evidence that employers are experiencing high turnover. Employers have difficulties recruiting workers with needed skills. These difficulties are not explained solely by the skills shortage. An ambitious 2006

Table 6.1   Most Important Factors Affecting Women's Participation in the Labor Force, by Gender
(percent)

Factor	Women	Men
Proximity to home	19	25
Good transportation	18	21
Suitable hours	18	11
Good pay	17	20
Suitable career	14	9
Availability of on-site nursery	8	8
Health care and social security insurance	3	2
Part-time work possible	2	2
Other	1	0
Ability to leave baby with family	0	0

Source: World Bank 2008c.

announcement of training opportunities in the textile sector failed to attract job applicants.[1] The poor work environment in the textile sector may partially explain workers' reluctance to apply for these job-linked training opportunities. This evidence suggests the need to address the working environment for all employees. Because female workers are more adversely affected, female-friendly work environments and policies should also be promoted through outreach campaigns and discussions with employers' organizations.

Increasing Women's Access to Finance, Including through Microcredit

Women's lack of access to bank financing could be addressed by encouraging banks to recognize the value of female customers. Various institutions in both developed and developing countries have started addressing women's limited access to finance through the development of innovative schemes and banking products. Some of these schemes have been implemented in Egypt; their expansion to a much broader range of women could help meet the continued need. Commercial banks should be made aware of the commercial opportunity that women present and encouraged to develop programs targeting female customers. These programs should be coupled with training on business and financial literacy for female clients.

Microfinance could help meet the needs of poorer women, helping enhance their overall well-being and economic security. Its use is not widespread in Egypt, but there are new opportunities. The World Bank's Enhancing Access to Finance for Micro and Small Enterprises project, which is currently being designed for Egypt, would help fill the significant gap in microcredit provision. To ensure broad coverage, the project should ensure geographic reach to underserved areas of the country. It should integrate sex-specific concerns into its design, implementing them by putting in place sex-specific targets and ensuring that women are designated as beneficiaries of any training and technical assistance. Research on microfinance should include sex-disaggregated analysis, so that programs and related training can be tailored to female clients' needs.

In addition to expanding microcredit coverage, the government could improve the broader regulatory and business environment for the provision of credit. Improving credit information legislation has helped improve the information exchange between financial institutions in other countries. The government's recent efforts on this front through iScore are encouraging.

Enhancing Vocational Training for Girls and Training for Female Workers

Human capital investments in girls are likely to have lifelong consequences for enhancing gender equity. Although the Middle East and North Africa region has made great strides in achieving gender parity in primary education, too many girls—especially girls from poor, rural families—are dropping out of school to perform paid or unpaid domestic labor in Egypt. Public support for school- and community-based childcare has the potential to provide young women with a broader range of labor market options than are currently available.

Although access to training is very limited for both men and women, women face far fewer training opportunities than do men in Egypt. Almost half of firms that employ women and offer training for their employees do not train a single woman. Special incentives—such as those provided through the granting of the Gender Equity Seal model developed in Mexico and replicated as a pilot in Egypt with World Bank assistance (box 6.1)—could help encourage firms to ensure that women have equitable access to training opportunities. Disseminating best practices and highlighting the business case for training could also help raise awareness among firms of the benefits of a well-trained female workforce.

Box 6.1

The Gender Equity Model

To encourage women's participation in Egypt's labor market, the government partnered with the World Bank on a pilot gender equity model in 2007. First developed in Mexico, the program promotes gender equality in private firms by developing a certification process for firms that take certain actions. Certified firms receive a seal and broad recognition through a public campaign. After the program in Mexico produced numerous positive results, the government of Egypt expressed interest in replicating it. The aim is to produce voluntary certification and training to firms that put in place policies on gender equity in staff recruitment, training, career development, and sexual harassment prevention.

Source: Castro 2007.

Conducting Research and Sex-Disaggregated Analysis of the Work Environment

Although this report provides a useful starting point, more data collection and analysis is needed. These efforts should look beyond the formal sector by examining women's self-employment and home-based entrepreneurship. Analysis of the determinants of productivity in firms finds that firms that employ more women are no more or less productive on average than other firms. The reason why certain firms and sectors exclude women from employment remains therefore unclear. Additional research on the costs of employing women relative to men would help shed light on this issue.

Approaches such as audit studies that send equally qualified male and female candidates on job interviews or send matched resumes in response to job postings will be needed to examine the degree to which custom, prejudice, and discrimination exclude women from employment in Egypt. Focus group analyses with employers are also powerful for eliciting information on employers' attitudes toward the recruitment, hiring, training, and promotion of women.

The reforms proposed in this chapter have the potential to significantly improve the environment for working women in Egypt. Doing so would not only benefit the women and their families, but also contribute to the overall economic well-being of the country.

Note

1. The training program targeted the training and employment of 27,000 workers. The call for trainees managed to attract just 77 percent of the target by September 2006; special efforts were needed to meet the target.

Characteristics of Surveyed Workers

This appendix—and much of the data in the main report—is based on data from the World Bank Investment Climate Survey (ICS), the ICS recall survey, and a Gender Workers Module. The ICS of 1,156 enterprises from the manufacturing sector was carried out in October 2008, using the World Bank standard methodology. The recall questionnaire of 566 enterprises was conducted in October 2008. The Gender Workers Module was conducted in August 2005. It sampled about 15 full-time workers from each firm covered by the ICS recall survey. About 70 percent of the sample is made up of small and medium firms, about 85 percent of which are owned by individuals or families. Large firms—firms employing more than 150 workers—account for about 30 percent of the sample.

Demographic Characteristics

Females enter the labor market earlier than males (table A.1): 15 percent of working women and just 5 percent of male workers are under the age of 20. Almost half of working women are 20–29, and another 31 percent are 30–49. This age distribution reflects the fact that women tend to work when they do not need to attend to young children. About two-thirds of the women interviewed were single, engaged, or preparing to

Table A.1   Demographic Characteristics of Male and Female Surveyed Workers

(percent)

Characteristic	Male	Female
Age		
Less than 20	4.9	14.6
20–29	28.2	49.6
30–39	32.1	16.9
40–49	21.9	14.0
50–59	11.0	4.7
60–69	1.3	–
More than 69	0.5	0.2
Marital status		
Married	72.3	27.5
Single	20.5	48.7
Engaged	5.0	15.8
Separated	0.2	0.3
Divorced	0.4	3.3
Widowed	0.5	2.7
Number of times married		
Once	96.4	98.6
More than once	3.6	1.4

Source: Authors, based on data from the Gender Workers Module.
Note: Based on sample of 2,593 men and 642 women.

get married. Just 28 percent of female workers were married; 6 percent were divorced or widowed. Women entered work earlier and stayed for a shorter period than men.

The percentage of male workers increases with age through 30–39 (31 percent) then decreases (at a lower rate than for female workers). In stark contrast to women, 72 percent of male workers were married at the time of interview. Only 27 percent were single or engaged; 1 percent were divorced or widowed. Male workers were more likely than their female counterparts to marry more than once.

Socioeconomic Characteristics

The level of education was higher among female workers: 47 percent of female workers and 42 percent of male workers completed at least secondary school (table A.2). Seventeen percent of male workers and 15 percent of female workers were illiterate. Only 7 percent of both male and female workers reported having either a savings or a checking account.

Table A.2   Socioeconomic Characteristics of Male and Female Surveyed Workers
(percent)

Characteristic	Male	Female
Education[a]		
No education	10.1	8.4
Primary	20.3	14.5
Preparatory	14.6	19.4
Secondary	3.6	5.8
Above secondary	32.1	35.3
University graduate and higher	5.9	5.2
Literacy		
Literate	83.2	84.8
Illiterate	16.8	15.2
Bank account		
Checking account	4.2	2.7
Savings account/profit & loss	3.9	5.5

Source: Authors, based on data from the Gender Workers Module.
Note: Based on sample of 2,609 men and 645 women.
a. Basic education (ages 4–14) includes kindergarten, six years of primary school, and three years of preparatory school. Secondary school lasts three years (ages 15–17).

Housing Characteristics

Almost three-quarters of male and female workers live in apartments; 18 percent live in houses (table A.3). Gender differences are not significant. Female workers are more likely than male workers to live in a rented residence rather than one they own.

Almost all workers, male and female, live in dwellings with electricity, and nearly 90 percent have access to piped water, mainly connected to their house. Male workers are somewhat more likely to have a modern flush toilet (54 percent) than a traditional toilet (46 percent). In comparison, 43 percent of female workers report having a modern flush toilet and 57 percent report having a traditional toilet. About three-quarters of male and female workers live in dwellings with cement tile floors, 10 percent live in dwellings with cement floors, and 8 percent live in dwelling with ceramic floors. Nearly all workers have separate bathrooms (97 percent) and kitchens (94 percent).

Household Possessions

As household possessions are an indicator for the standard of living, workers were asked about their possessions of some durable goods and other

Table A.3   Housing of Male and Female Surveyed Workers
(percent)

Characteristic	Male	Female
Type of residence		
Apartment in a building	76.1	79.6
Separate house	18.5	17.3
Part of house	3.6	0.9
Separate room	1.2	1.6
Common residence for workers	1.2	0.1
Villa	0.5	0.4
Ownership of residence		
Rented	47.1	53.0
Owned by the household	48.9	43.2
Common ownership	3.3	3.5
Legal status		
Old law	23.3	15.0
New law	76.7	85.0
Type of new law rent[a]		
Specific period	58.8	56.1
Open period	41.2	43.9
Source of electricity		
Public network	99.5	99.4
Generator	0.2	0.4
Source of drinking water		
Pipes connected to the house	91.2	95.2
Pump	5.2	1.5
Faucet from neighbors	0.5	1.5
Public faucet	1.1	0.7
Common faucet in a building	0.7	0.5
Well	0.0	0
Canal/Nile	1.2	0
Sanitation facilities		
Modern flush toilet	54.1	43.1
Traditional type	45.8	56.7
Hole	0.1	0.2
Kitchen or a place for cooking only	94.2	94.1
Flooring		
Cement tiles	76.2	78.6
Ceramics/marble tiles	7.1	7.9
Cement	10.0	8.7
Earth/sand	3.7	2.7
Parquet	0.1	2.7
Wall-to-wall carpet	2.6	1.2
Canaltex	0.1	0.8
Linoleum	0.1	0

(continued)

Table A.3   Housing of Male and Female Surveyed Workers
(percent) (Continued)

Characteristic	Male	Female
Bathroom separated / common		
Separate	96.9	96.8
Common	3.0	3.0
Bathroom connection		
Public drainage network	77.7	87.3
Trench drained from time to time	20.5	12.2
Drainage/canal	0.8	0.1
Well drained into the ground	0.9	0

Source: Authors, based on data from the Gender Workers Module.
Note: a. Egypt's tenant laws have undergone a series of changes over the decades. Rent increases are highly unlikely in tenancies governed by the old socialist laws (Law No. 49/1977, Law No. 136/1981, or earlier legislation). These laws apply to contracts entered into before the reforms of 1996, when new legislation comprehensively deregulated landlord and tenant relationships. Rents can be for a fixed term (usually three to five years) or open.

possessions. With regard to durable goods, differences between male and female workers are minimal: about 9 in 10 workers own burners and refrigerators; 8 in 10 own radio/tape players, electric fans, and ordinary washing machines; 7 in 10 own a color TV; 3 in 10 own gas burners, cooking stoves, and real estate (land or buildings); and 2 in 10 own automatic washing machines and black and white TVs (table A.4).

Occupation
The majority of both men (63 percent) and women (56 percent) are production workers (table A.5). Women are more likely than men to work as administrative workers (12 percent of women, less than 9 percent of men). Fifty percent of male workers and 40 percent of female workers reported being formally registered in their enterprise as full-time workers. Among those workers, 72 percent of male and 69 of female workers had been registered in their enterprise since the beginning of work. Females are more likely than males to work without registration (56 percent of females are not registered compared with 46 percent of males).

Challenges Facing Working Women
The survey asked enterprise managers about the advantages and disadvantages of hiring women (table A.6). Forty-two percent indicated that there is no advantage to hiring woman in their enterprises; 15 percent mentioned that women are more productive and more caring than men;

Table A.4   Household Possessions of Male and Female Surveyed Workers
(percent)

Asset	Male	Female
Household appliance		
Burner	92.8	94.9
Refrigerator	87.8	93.0
Ordinary washing machine	80.7	79.4
Cooking stove	29.4	36.1
Gas burner	24.1	30.5
Fully automatic washing machine	21.2	22.6
Sewing machine	9.8	20.0
Deep freezer	4.0	6.7
Microwave oven	2.1	2.9
Heating and air conditioning		
Electric fan	81.2	81.6
Heater	38.6	38.8
Air conditioner	2.3	3.6
Electronic appliance		
Radio/tape player	87.8	87.1
Color TV	78.4	78.9
Black and white TV	21.7	22.6
Transportation		
Bicycle	11.7	7.0
Private car	3.4	4.6
Truck	0.4	0.7
Taxicab	0.2	0.5
Motorcycle	1.0	0.1
Information and communication technology		
Telephone (landline)	46.2	52.5
Mobile phone	22.5	27.5
Computer	8.8	11.8
Fax machine	12.4	18.2
Video player	8.7	14.2
Land		
Agricultural land	5.6	5.6
Real estate (land or buildings)	29.9	30.9
Rent a piece of land	1.2	1.0
Sharecropping	0.2	0.3

Source: Authors, based on data from the Gender Workers Module.
Note: Results show ownership of or access to item within the household.

Table A.5   Type of Job and Registration Status of Surveyed Male and Female Workers

(percent)

Item	Male	Female
Occupation		
Production worker	63.3	55.5
Nonproduction worker	18.2	24.1
Administration	8.6	12.0
Professional	9.5	8.3
Trainee	0.0	0.1
Registered in this enterprise		
As full-time employee	50.1	40.7
Registered since beginning of employment	71.9	69.0
As temporary employee	3.5	3.2
Not registered	46.4	56.1

Source: Authors, based on data from the Gender Workers Module.

Table A.6   Managers' Positive Perceptions of Women

Perception	Percent of managers
Women are more productive and more caring than men are	14.7
Women are more trustworthy than men are	8.1
Hiring a woman costs less than employing a man	8.4
Women have same qualifications as men but better training	5.8
Women are absent less often than men are	2.5
Other	18.3
No advantage	42.1

Source: Authors, based on data from the Gender Workers Module.

8 percent reported that employing women costs them than employing men; and 8 percent said that women are more trustworthy than men.

There were also some negative perceptions toward women (table A.7). Twenty-one percent of managers complained that maternity issues affect women's work, 18 percent reported that women are less committed to their work than men, and 14 percent mentioned that women were absent too frequently.

Managers were asked for suggestions on facilitating women working (table A.8). One-third (32 percent) reported that nothing can be done to make it easier for women to work easier, 23 percent cited a part-time work, 13 percent cited availability of nearby daycare facilities, and almost 5 percent cited piecemeal payment.

Table A.7   Managers' Negative Perceptions of Women

Perception	Percent of managers
Marriage and maternity affect women's work	20.5
Women are less committed to work than men are	18.1
Women are unable to perform hard work	14.2
Women are absent more often than men are	14.0
Women quit more than men do	11.0
Women cannot work overtime or extra hours	6.8
Nature of work is not suitable for women	6.4
Women are less productive than men are	3.3
Women have the same qualifications as men but less training	1.8
Women are less trustworthy than men are	1.3
Women's work is not accurate enough	1.0
Other	1.5

Source: Authors, based on data from the Gender Workers Module.

Table A.8   Managers' Suggestions for Making It Easier for Women to Work

Suggestion	Percent of managers
Availability of part-time employment	22.8
Availability of nearby daycare centers	12.6
Availability of piecework payment according to productivity	4.5
Husband should participate in home duties	3.5
More training	3.5
Other	15.6
Not applicable	5.7
None	31.9

Source: Authors, based on data from the Gender Workers Module.

References

Abdelhadi, Magdi. 2008. "Egypt's Sexual Harassment 'Cancer.'" July 18. BBC News, London.

Al-Ayram Weekly. 2007. "Women in Business." March 8–14. http://weekly.ahram .org.eg/2007/835/sc63.htm.

Al-Bassusi, Nagah Hassan, and Safaa El-Tayeb El-Kogali. 2001. *Youth Livelihoods Opportunities in Egypt*. Cairo: Population Council.

Anker, Richard. 1998. *Gender and Jobs: Sex Segregation of Occupations in the World*. Geneva: International Labour Organization.

Anker, Richard., and Catherine Hein. 1986. *Inequalities in Urban Employment in the Third World*. London: Macmillan.

Anker, Richard, Helina Melkas, and Ailsa Korten. 2003. "Gender-Based Occupational Segregation in the 1990s." Focus Programme on Promoting the Declaration on Fundamental Principles and Rights at Work, Work in Freedom, Working Paper 16, International Labour Organization, Geneva.

Assaad, Ragui. 2002. "The Transformation of the Egyptian Labor Market." In *Egyptian Labor Market in an Era of Reform*, ed. R. Assaad. Cairo: Economic Research Forum.

Awumbila, Mariama., and J. H. Monsen. 1995. "Gender and the Environment: Women's Time Use as Measure of Environmental Change." *Global Environment Change* 5 (4): 337–46.

Bakir, Sherine. 2005. "A Constant Pull." *Business Today*. November. Available at: http://www.businesstodayegypt.com/article.aspx?ArticleID=6075.

Bollen, Kenneth A., and Robert W. Jackman. 1990. "Regression Diagnostics: An Expository Treatment of Outliers and Influential Cases." In *Modern Methods of Data Analysis*, ed. J. Fox and J. S. Long, 257–91. Newbury Park, CA: Sage.

CAPMAS. 2008. Labor Force Sample Survey 1995, 2000, 2005, 2006, and 2007. CAPMAS, Cairo.

Castro, Maria Elena. 2007. *Gender Equity Promotion in the Private Sector in Mexico: The Development of a Successful Model.* SmartLessons in Advisory Services. Washington, DC: International Finance Corporation.

Chamlou, Nadereh, Leora Klapper, and Silvia Muzi. 2008. *The Environment for Women's Entrepreneurship in the Middle East and North Africa.* Washington, DC: World Bank.

Cutura, Jozefina. 2009. *Promoting Women's Economic Empowerment: The Learning Journey of Standard Chartered Bank.* Private Sector Leaders Forum, World Bank, Washington, DC.

El-Kogali, Safaa. 2000. *For Better or for Worse? The Status of Women in the Labor Market in Egypt, 1988–1998.* Economic Research Forum for the Arab Countries, Iran and Turkey, Egypt Labor Market Project. World Bank, Washington, DC.

Ellis, Amanda, Claire Manuel, and Mark Blackden. 2006. *Gender and Economic Growth in Uganda: Unleashing the Power of Women.* Directions in Development Serieas. Washington, DC: World Bank.

El-Mahdi, Alia, and Mona Amer. 2005. "Egypt: Growing Informality 1993–2003." In *Good Jobs, Bad Jobs, No Jobs: Labor Markets and Informal Work in Egypt, El Salvador, India, Russia, and South Africa*, ed. T. Avirgan, S. Gammage, and J. Bivens. Washington, DC: Global Policy Network, Economic Policy Institute.

Fain, James. 1998. "The Causes and Consequences of Occupational Segregation: A Simultaneous Equations Approach." *Applied Economics* 30 (10): 1361–67.

Filer, Randall K. 1985. "Male-Female Differences: The Importance of Compensating Differentials." *Industrial and Labor Relations Review* 38 (3): 426–37.

Grameen Foundation (http://www.grameenfoundation.org/).

IFC (International Finance Corporation). 2007. "GEM Country Brief: Egypt 2007." Gender Entrepreneurship Markets, Washington, DC.

JICA. 2005. "Study on Gender and Socio-Cultural Diversity: Case Study in Egypt." Department of Planning and Coordination, JICA, Tokyo.

Klasen, Stephan. 2002. "Low Schooling for Girls, Slower Growth for All?" *World Bank Economic Review* 16: 345–73.

Klasen, Stephan, and Francesca Lamanna. 2008. "The Impact of Gender Inequality in Education and Employment on Economic Growth in Developing Countries: Updates and Extensions." Ibero America Institute for Economic Research (IAI), Discussion Paper 175, IAI.

Lamanna, Francesca, and Andrew Morrison. 2006. "Gender Issues in the Kyrgyz Labor Market." World Bank Working Paper, Europe and Central Asia Region, Washington, DC.

Mduma, John. 2005. "Gender Difference of Rural Off-Farm Employment Participation in Tanzania. Is Spatial Mobility An Issue?" University of Dar es Salaam.

Nasr, Sahar. 2008. *Access to Finance and Economic Growth in Egypt.* Washington, DC: World Bank, Middle East and North Africa Region.

Pérotin, Virginie, Andrew Robinson, and Joanne Loundes. 2003. "Equal Opportunities Practices and Enterprises Performance: An Investigation on Australian and British Data." Focus Programme on Promoting the Declaration on Fundamental Principles and Rights at Work, Work in Freedom, Working Paper 14, International Labour Organization, Geneva.

Pitts, Melinda. 2003. "Why Choose Women's Work If It Pays Less? A Structural Model of Occupational Choice." *Worker Well-Being and Public Policy, Research in Labor Economics* 22: 415–45.

Polachek, Solomon. 1981. "Occupational Self-Selection: A Human Capital Approach to Sex Differences in the Occupational Structure." *Review of Economics and Statistics* 63 (1): 60–69.

Saito, Katrine, Hailu Mekonnen, and Daphne Spurling. 1994. *Raising the Productivity of Women Farmers in Sub-Saharan Africa.* World Bank Discussion Paper 230, Washington, DC.

UNDP (United Nations Development Programme). 2008. *Egypt Human Development Report.* Cairo: UNDP and the Institute of Development Planning,

Wooldridge, J. M. 2002. *Econometric Analysis of Cross Section and Panel Data.* Cambridge, MA and London: The MIT Press.

World Bank Enterprise Surveys. Available at: http://www.enterprisesurveys.org/.

World Bank. 2003. *Egypt Country Gender Assessment.* Washington, DC: World Bank, Middle East and North Africa Region, Social and Economic Development Group.

———. 2004. *Gender and Development in the Middle East and North Africa: Women in the Public Sphere.* MENA Development Report. Washington, DC: World Bank, Middle East and North Africa Region.

———. 2005. *Country Assistance Strategy for the Arab Republic of Egypt FY06–FY09.* Washington, DC: World Bank, Middle East and North Africa Region.

————. 2007a. *Access to Finance and Economic Growth in Egypt*. Washington, DC: World Bank, Middle East and North Africa Region.

————. 2007b. *Chile Country Gender Assessment*. Washington, DC: World Bank, Latin America and the Caribbean Region.

————. 2007c. *Doing Business 2008*. Washington, DC: World Bank.

————. 2007d. *The Environment for Women's Entrepreneurship in the Middle East and North Africa Region*. Washington, DC: World Bank, Middle East and North Africa Region.

————. 2008a. *Doing Business 2009*. Washington, DC: World Bank.

————. 2008b. *Doing Business in the Arab World 2009*. Washington, DC: World Bank.

————. 2008c. *Egypt Investment Climate Survey*. Washington, DC: World Bank.

————. 2009a. *Doing Business 2010*. Washington, DC: World Bank.

————. 2009b. *Enhancing Access to Finance for Micro and Small Enterprises Concept Note*. Washington, DC: World Bank, Middle East and North Africa Region, Social and Economic Development Group.

————. 2009c. *Project Information Document: Enhancing Access to Finance for Micro and Small Enterprises*. Washington, DC: World Bank, Middle East and North Africa Region, Social and Economic Development Group.

Index

Figures, notes, and tables are indicated by *f*, *n*, and *t*, respectively.

ECO-AUDIT
Environmental Benefits Statement

The World Bank is committed to preserving endangered forests and natural resources. The Office of the Publisher has chosen to print *Egyptian Women Workers and Entrepreneurs* on recycled paper with 50 percent post-consumer waste, in accordance with the recommended standards for paper usage set by the Green Press Initiative, a nonprofit program supporting publishers in using fiber that is not sourced from endangered forests. For more information, visit www.greenpressinitia-

Saved:
- 3 trees
- 1 million BTU's of total energy
- 252 lbs. of CO_2 equivalent of greenhouse gases
- 1,214 gallons of waste water
- 74 lbs. of solid waste

green
press
INITIATIVE

www.ingramcontent.com/pod-product-compliance
Lightning Source LLC
Chambersburg PA
CBHW062043270326
41929CB00014B/2525